Irene Artes Hedlin

The Individual in a New Society:
A Study of Selected "Erzählungen" and "Kurzgeschichten"
of the German Democratic Republic from 1965 to 1972

Kanadische Studien zur deutschen Sprache und Literatur

Etudes parues au Canada en relation
avec la philologie et la littérature allemandes

Canadian Studies in German Language and Literature

herausgegeben von
Armin Arnold · Michael S. Batts · Hans Eichner

Nr. 16

Irene Artes Hedlin

The Individual in a New Society:
A Study of Selected «Erzählungen» and «Kurzgeschichten»
of the German Democratic Republic from 1965 to 1972

Peter Lang
Bern · Frankfurt am Main · Las Vegas
1977

Irene Artes Hedlin

The Individual
in a New Society

A Study of Selected «Erzählungen» and «Kurzgeschichten»
of the German Democratic Republic from 1965 to 1972

Peter Lang
Bern · Frankfurt am Main · Las Vegas
1977

ISBN 3 261 02094 6

© Verlag Peter Lang, Bern 1977
Nachfolger des Verlages der
Herbert Lang & Cie AG, Bern
Alle Rechte vorbehalten.

Nachdruck oder Vervielfältigung, auch auszugsweise, in allen Formen wie
Mikrofilm, Xerographie, Mikrofiche, Mikrocard, Offset verboten.

Druck: Lang Druck AG, Liebefeld/Bern

CONTENTS

INTRODUCTION

The individual in a new society is a dominant theme in the literature of the German Democratic Republic (GDR).[1] This fact is particularly true of more recent literature, especially that written after 1965. A large number of works of fiction written in that country deal with the every-day life of the individual in socialist society, particularly his relationship to his work, to the collective, and to his family and friends. Frequently, the main character is a worker: a member of a brigade at a construction site, a farmer in a *Landwirtschaftliche Produktionsgenossenschaft* (LPG),[2] or an emancipated woman actively engaged in some facet of economic production. Other characters are portrayed as trying to become a part of the new society: an old man trying to discover how he may contribute to it in some useful way, or a youth trying to find his identity within the larger whole. "Ich glaube, daß die Darstellung der Wechselbeziehung Individuum-Gesellschaft das eigentliche Feld der Literatur ist,"[3] observed Werner Heiduczek, an East German author, in an interview.

The mode of writing known as socialist realism, which particularly emphasizes the working class and the building-up of a socialist society as the proper subject matter of literature, has led the writers of the GDR to portray the worker and his life in their narrative prose works. To enable them to understand the needs and concerns of the workers more fully, they were encouraged to join them at their place of work and to share their experiences. In fact, in April 1959, the First Bitterfeld Conference, held in the Cultural Palace of the huge chemical plant in the town of Bitterfeld, was called for the purpose of making writers more aware of the concerns of the workers, and, at the same time, of encouraging workers to write about their own experiences. Thus, an effort was made to bridge the gap between art and life, to develop the artistic life of the working class, and to involve the writer more and more in the problems of the worker.

Walter Ulbricht, in his closing speech at this conference, stressed the concern of the Party to make the worker and his relationships in socialist society the main subject of prose fiction. The task of the writer is the portrayal of the new society; he said: "Wir sind der Meinung, daß es gerade *die*

Periodicals are abbreviated according to the Master List and Table of Abbreviations in the International Bibliography of *Publications of the Modern Language Association of America.*

[1] The geographical term "East Germany" and the abbreviation "GDR" for the official political designation "German Democratic Republic" will be used interchangeably throughout the text.
[2] This is the designation for a collective farm in the GDR. It is most commonly referred to as "LPG," and this abbreviation will be used throughout the text.
[3] Heinz Plavius, "Gespräch mit Werner Heiduczek," *NDL,* 19, No. 8 (1971), 20.

Gegenwartsaufgabe des Schriftstellers ist, das Neue in der gegenwärtigen
sozialistischen Umgestaltung, in der Entwicklung des gesamten wirtschaftlichen
und kulturellen Lebens, der neuen Beziehungen der Menschen, des neuen
gesellschaftlichen Lebens zu gestalten."[4] Eva Strittmatter reinforces this view
when she observes in her essay "Literatur und Wirklichkeit" that since the First
Bitterfeld Conference, the presentation of current themes and events and the
portrayal of the interaction and unity of personal and social life in socialism
have become a necessity of life (*Lebensbedürfnis*) to the majority of young
writers.[5] Thus, the theme of the individual in a new society has found a central
place in the literature of the GDR.

The sentiment that something completely new is being produced in the
literature of the GDR pervades the writings of East German literary critics and
of those who set the goals of the literature of the country. The critic Klaus
Jarmatz speaks of the development of "eine neue Literatur mit neuen Inhalten
und Funktionen, die der neuen Gesellschaft entsprechen . . . ,"[6] and the result
is, as Jarmatz calls it, "eine neue Literatur" (p. 17). The proper and suitable
new literature for the GDR is that which expresses a new view of man: "Die
unserer Gesellschaft angemessene Literatur gründet sich auf eine qualitativ neue
Menschenauffassung" (pp. 79–80). It also has the task of expressing and
revealing the new social structure: "Die sozialistische Literatur von heute hat
den neuen menschlichen Bezug unserer Gesellschaftsformation zu erschließen,
geht sie doch von einem neuen gesellschaftlichen Grunderlebnis aus . . ."
(p. 71). It is striking how often in this connection the word "new" appears in
the statements of Jarmatz, as well as in the passage from Walter Ulbricht's
speech quoted above.

However, not only is it a new literature as far as content is concerned,
though this may be its main characteristic, but the form, or rather, the method
or way of expressing the new content, too, is new. Jarmatz speaks of a
literature with a new subject matter and function, and also "mit neuen
Formen, die diesem Inhalt und dieser Funktion adäquat sind" (pp. 17–18).
The socialist cultural revolution, according to Jarmatz, leads to new aesthetic
principles which express the new social conditions. These principles are those
found in socialist realism.

---

[4] "Schlußwort zur 1. Bitterfelder Konferenz," in *Kritik in der Zeit: Der Sozialismus –
seine Literatur – ihre Entwicklung,* ed. Klaus Jarmatz (Halle/Saale: Mitteldeutscher Verlag,
1970), pp. 462–63.
[5] In *Kritik in der Zeit,* p. 500.
[6] "Kritik in der Zeit," in *Kritik in der Zeit,* p. 17.

Socialist realism

It is not the purpose of this study to expound the theories of socialist realism; this task has been dealt with in extensive special investigations.[7] However, a few of the main aspects should be considered briefly, since this is the theory of literature practised in socialist countries, and most of the better known writers of the GDR adhere to a greater or lesser degree to its tenets. It is, moreover, the officially approved mode of writing. Klaus Jarmatz states:

> 1957 und 1958 wurden Jahre entscheidender Klärungen. Die sozialistische Perspektive für die DDR und ihre Literatur wurden auf der Kulturkonferenz und auf dem V. Parteitag der SED klar bestimmt. Für die Literaturkritik konnte es keinen Zweifel geben, daß der sozialistische Realismus die den neuen gesellschaftlichen Verhältnissen adäquate künstlerische Gestaltungsmethode ist. (p. 63)

This statement shows that it is the result of official Party policy that socialist realism is the mode of writing used to portray life in the GDR.

Socialist realism goes back to the tradition of realistic writing of the Nineteenth Century. The man who officially proclaimed and set down its tenets in the Twentieth Century was Maxim Gorki. With his novel *Die Mutter* (1906), which marked "die Geburtsstunde der Kunst des sozialistischen Realismus,"[8] he set a successful example for this mode of writing. In his speech to the First All Union Congress of Soviet Writers in 1934, in which he stated that the true subject of literature is the labourer, he expressed its theory.

Another name frequently mentioned in connection with socialist realism is that of Friedrich Engels, even though what he has said is found in two letters, and thus the statements are of a casual and personal nature. In his letter to Margaret Harkness (London, April 1888), he writes: "Realismus bedeutet, meines Erachtens, außer der Treue des Details die getreue Wiedergabe typischer Charaktere unter typischen Umständen."[9] On the other hand, in the letter to Minna Kautsky (London, 26 November 1885), he speaks of the "treue Schilderung der wirklichen Verhältnisse" (ibid., p. 156). In the same letter the concept of *Tendenzpoesie* (p. 156) appears. Friedrich Engels thus valued realistic writing and faithfulness to detail, but at the same time spoke of the typical, a concept implying a generalization which is necessarily idealized. This contradiction is justified by the fact that he had *Tendenzpoesie* in mind, a literature with a special purpose, intended to serve socialist goals.

---

[7]   The most complete East German work on socialist realism to date is Erwin Pracht and Werner Neubert, eds., *Sozialistischer Realismus – Positionen, Probleme, Perspektiven: Eine Einführung* (Berlin: Dietz, 1970). (Hereafter cited as "Pracht and Neubert.")

[8]   Pracht and Neubert, p. 29.

[9]   Karl Marx and Friedrich Engels, *Über Kunst und Literatur in zwei Bänden,* Vol. 1 (Berlin: Dietz, 1967), p. 157.

Four terms which indicate some of the essential qualities and aspects of socialist realism are: *Parteilichkeit, Perspektive, Volksverbundenheit,* and *positiver Held. Parteilichkeit* means that the work of literature supports the goals of Marxism-Leninism. Pracht and Neubert observe: "Sozialistische Parteilichkeit bedeutet, daß der Künstler und sein Werk bewußt, und das heißt, offen, ehrlich und konsequent für die Idee des wissenschaftlichen Sozialismus eintritt" (p. 238). Therefore the writer must shape his work in terms of socialist thought and doctrine. A manual on writing states: "Genaue Kenntnis der Wirklichkeit genügt keineswegs. Der Schriftsteller muß seiner Welt wertend und parteilich gegenüberstehen."[10] In other words, realistic depiction is only part of the writer's task; he must present the world as seen by socialism.

Socialist realism also reveals *Perspektive,* which means seeing reality in terms of the future,[11] of what it will become through socialism; it is "die Notwendigkeit, im Heute schon das Morgen zu entdecken . . ."[12] Thus, in socialist realism, the writer is asked to portray the world as it is, and, at the same time, as it will become in socialism; it has to be presented from a specific point of view, "als eine den Sozialismus aufbauende Welt."[13] This fact is brought out quite clearly in the four basic principles of socialist realism set down by Anna Seghers. She says: one, that the writer should present the world as it is, namely as one in which socialism is being built up; secondly, that this means a world that is moving forward; thirdly, that the writer should have the ability to narrate; and finally, that he should present reality from a specific aspect, so as to arouse in the reader the desire to take part in the work of creating the new world (ibid., pp. 80–81). Thus, socialist realism, though it portrays every-day life and events, presents them from the specific point of view of socialism, and in terms of the future as it is envisioned by it.

The protagonist of such a work is a "positive hero" (*positiver Held*), for the characters are seen in an idealized way and presented as examples to be emulated. Furthermore, *Volksverbundenheit,* or solidarity with the people, is essential. Thus the hero is a worker, and the language and setting are generally those of the working class. Popular themes that would appeal to the greatest number are presented, and usually any literary experimentation is avoided. It is important that the people find their problems portrayed in a work of literature, and, moreover, that they be presented in a way easily understood by all. Pracht and Neubert observe:

---

[10]   *Literaturkunde: Beiträge zu Wesen und Formen der Dichtung,* 3rd ed., rev. (Leipzig: Fachbuchverlag, 1965), p. 17.
[11]   The usually neutral term *Perspektive* has been narrowed down to mean *Zukunftsperspektive* in the usage of the GDR, where it has become a key word.
[12]   Pracht and Neubert, p. 86.
[13]   Anna Seghers, "Bewahrung und Entdeckung," *NDL,* 11, No. 8 (1963), 56, quoted by Jarmatz in "Kritik in der Zeit," in *Kritik in der Zeit,* p. 80.

Damit die Kunst des sozialistischen Realismus ihrer Funktion in vollem Maße gerecht zu werden vermag, nämlich Beitrag zur Selbstverständigung des Volkes über seine Leistungen, seine Aufgaben und seine Probleme zu sein, muß sie Zugang zum Volk finden, muß sie es 'zu packen', 'anzusprechen' wissen. (p. 215)

Socialist realism has a function to perform; it has to appeal to, and identify with, the masses. Karin Thomas, a West German critic, defines the function of the writer of socialist realism more explicitly when she says that this literature "wendet sich nicht mehr an das aufgeklärte Individuum, sondern an die breite Masse des Proletariats ... um als parteipolitisches Erziehungsinstrument für Aufbauarbeit und Kollektivierung wirksam zu sein."[14]

Literature with a purpose

From what has been said so far, it becomes evident that the literature of the GDR is, above all else, a literature with a purpose, committed to the goals of socialism and the society to be created by it. The government and the writers of the GDR chose socialist realism because it serves their purposes best. Writers feel that they have been given a definite task by the society and the state, which publishes their works. Pracht and Neubert make the following fundamental assumption: "Eine Trennung von Kunst, künstlerischem Schaffen und Politik ist für den sozialistischen Realisten ... völlig unvereinbar" (p. 239).

The policy of using literature as an instrument in the development of socialist society has been put into practice by the *Sozialistische Einheitspartei Deutschlands* (SED) since the founding of the republic on October 7, 1949. One of the statements made at the first Party Conference of the SED in 1949 stresses the importance of literature, and of art in general, in relation to this task:

Die kulturelle Aufgabe, Menschen mit einer neuen gesellschaftlichen Erkenntnis und einer neuen Einstellung zur Arbeit zu erziehen, ist nur zu erfüllen, wenn alle Schriftsteller und Künstler ihre ganze Kraft und Begeisterung diesem Werk widmen.[15]

The writer is given the task of developing a new consciousness in his readers, and of creating in them a joy in work and a feeling of optimism: "Die fortschrittlichen Schriftsteller können durch ihre Werke dazu beitragen, Arbeitsfreude und Optimismus bei den Arbeitern in den Betrieben und bei der

---

[14] "Die Literatur der DDR als Spiegel von Gesellschaftsbewußtsein und Gesellschaftskritik," in *Wissenschaft und Gesellschaft in der DDR,* ed. Peter C. Ludz (München: Hanser, 1971), p. 258.
[15] "Kulturelle Aufgaben im Rahmen des Zweijahrplanes: Entschließung der 1. Parteikonferenz der SED (Auszug)," in *Kritik in der Zeit,* p. 147.

werktätigen Landbevölkerung zu entwickeln" (ibid.). This statement, made by
the SED, shows how practical the contribution of the writer is expected to be.
Furthermore, writers are even given the themes they should present in their
literary works: "Die sozialistische Rekonstruktion und die Steigerung der
Arbeitsproduktivität, die Erreichung der Rentabilität in der sozialistischen
Landwirtschaft, die Entwicklung des sozialistischen Bewußtseins und der
sozialistischen Moral . . ."[16]

The words "Auftrag" and "Aufgabe" are used frequently in referring to the
socialist writer. Walter Ulbricht, speaking at the First Bitterfeld Conference,
sums up the task of the writer in the new society in the following words:

> Der Auftrag besteht darin, daß sie das Neue im Leben, in den gesellschaftlichen
> Beziehungen der Menschen, in ihrem Kampf um den sozialistischen Aufbau, um die
> sozialistische Umgestaltung des gesamten Lebens künstlerisch gestalten, daß sie durch
> ihre künstlerischen Leistungen die Menschen begeistern und dadurch mithelfen, das
> Tempo der Entwicklung zu beschleunigen und vorwärtszubringen.[17]

References like these to literature as an instrument of furthering the cause of
socialism and of advancing the productivity of the society occur again and
again in the literary criticism and theory of the GDR.

This fact implies that the literature of this country tries to help the
individual to shape his life in the socialist mould: "Die Grundfrage, die
Literatur mit beantworten hilft, ist: Wie soll man heute leben, wie kann man
heute leben? Diese Frage ist in den jüngsten Erscheinungen unserer Literatur
das stets wiederkehrende Hauptmotiv."[18] Accordingly, literature attempts not
only to further the aims of socialist society in a direct way, but also to deal
with the personal and moral problems of the individual. "Wir wünschen uns
Bücher . . . die den Menschen verständlich machen, in welcher Richtung, durch
alle Konflikte hindurch, die Lösung liegt,"[19] states Anna Seghers. She observes
that it is not enough to represent a conflict, but to present it in a certain way in
terms of *Perspektive*, i.e., the future seen in terms of socialism: "Es gehört zu
meinem Beruf, daß ich sowohl die Leute, die ich darstelle, wie die Leute, die
mich lesen, nicht ratlos sitzen lasse."[20] Thus Anna Seghers feels obliged to
offer direction and advice in her literary works. Similarly, the writer Helmut
Sakowski states: "Für mich ist die Machart nicht das Wichtigste . . . . Für mich
ist wichtig, daß eine Geschichte erzählt wird, die an den Nerv der Zeit rührt.

---

[16] Eva Strittmatter, "Literatur und Wirklichkeit," in *Kritik in der Zeit,* p. 507.
[17] Ulbricht, "Schlußwort zur 1. Bitterfelder Konferenz," in *Kritik in der Zeit,* p. 460.
[18] Pracht and Neubert, p. 203.
[19] "Die Tiefe und Breite in der Literatur," in *Kritik in der Zeit,* p. 493.
[20] Anna Seghers speaking at the Writers' Congress, Moscow, 15—26 December 1954,
quoted by Sigrid Bock, "Einleitung," in *Über Kunstwerk und Wirklichkeit,* by Anna Seghers,
3 vols. (Berlin: Akademie Verlag, 1970—71), I, 59.

Das wird immer eine moderne Geschichte sein. Welcher Mittel ich mich dabei bediene, das ist für mich zweitrangig."[21] Thus content is the chief criterion for him as well.

The short narrative prose forms in the GDR

In spite of the fact that strong emphasis is placed on content and ideology, some interest in form is also apparent among literary critics and writers. Although Anna Seghers, for example, is concerned primarily with ideology, she does admit: "Das richtige Thema bürgt nicht allein für den Wert, auch wenn es noch so gewaltig wäre. Erst seine richtige Darstellung."[22] Sigrid Bock, in commenting on this statement, says:

> Es geht z.B. in der Beurteilung des literarischen Menschenbildes in Erzählungen und Novellen nicht darum, nur allgemein-philosophische und politisch-moralische Fragen zu erörtern. Sondern die *ästhetische* Spezifik eines *epischen* Helden in einer Erzählung oder Novelle muß sichtbar werden.[23]

She suggests the necessity for skill in creating literary characters, not just the importance of giving expression to the philosophical and political content of a literary work.

There is an increasing awareness and consciousness of literary form. More use is being made of the variety of literary forms, and, as Pracht and Neubert point out, greater attention is being paid to the specific qualities and characteristics of the various genres (p. 205). A number of critics mention the emerging popularity of the short prose forms. Werner Heiduczek notes: "Es ist bei uns zur Zeit modern geworden, die Bedeutung der kurzen epischen Form gegenüber ihrer bisherigen Vernachlässigung hervorzuheben."[24] Heinz Plavius observes, that even if there might have been a time, "da in der DDR-Literatur die kleine Form keine besondere Rolle spielte, so kann für die unmittelbare Gegenwart konstatiert werden, daß sich hier eine Wendung zum Besseren abzeichnet."[25]

The number of writers of *Erzählungen* and other short prose has increased very much since 1965. Whereas before that year, Franz Fühmann and Anna Seghers were the best known writers of *Erzählungen,* there are many recent

---

[21]   Volker Kurzweg, "Interview mit Helmut Sakowski," *WB,* 15, No. 4 (1969), 749.

[22]   "Die Tiefe und Breite in der Literatur," in *Kritik in der Zeit,* p. 488.

[23]   "Probleme des Menschenbildes in Erzählungen und Novellen (Beitrag zur Geschichte der sozialistisch-realistischen Erzählkunst in der DDR von 1956/57 bis 1963)," Diss. Institut für Gesellschaftswissenschaften beim ZK der SED, Berlin, 1964, p. iv.

[24]   Plavius, "Gespräch mit Werner Heiduczek," p. 22.

[25]   "Gestalt und Gestaltung . . . ," *NDL,* 16, No. 3 (1968), 151.

writers like Werner Bräunig, Manfred Jendryschik, Erik Neutsch, Joachim Nowotny and Siegfried Pitschmann, who have devoted themselves almost exclusively to the short narrative prose forms, and there are many others of whose works the *Erzählung* and related genres form a considerable part, as, for example, Jurij Brězan and Günter Kunert.

Among the reading public, too, a greater interest in the smaller genres is apparent. In her article "Laudatio auf die kleine Form," Renate Drenkow claims:

> Möglicherweise kann heute ein Schriftsteller auch mit einem steigenden gesellschaft-lichen Bedürfnis nach kurzer Prosa rechnen. Vermutlich ruft die sich im raschen Tempo vollziehende wissenschaftlich-technische Revolution mit ihrem ungeheuren Informationsfluß ein Bedürfnis nach 'ästhetischer Kurzinformation' hervor.[26]

Thus, there is an increase in the popularity of the shorter narrative forms both among writers and the reading public.

At the same time these forms are still chiefly looked upon as having a special contribution to make in helping to shape the new society and the socialist personality. For example, in a *Handbuch für schreibende Arbeiter* the following observation is made: "Gerade die epischen Kurzformen, die Anekdote, die Kurzgeschichte, aber auch die kleine Erzählung, sind äußerst wirksame Mittel, den Prozeß der Menschwerdung des Menschen, die Herausbil-dung sozialistischer Persönlichkeiten aktiv zu fördern."[27] Their effectiveness in reaching a large number of the public is valued: "Kurze epische Formen sind massenwirksame Formen. Die Presse hungert nach ihnen" (ibid.). Thus, their contribution in meeting the requirements of committed literature is taken into consideration first.

The popular Erzählung

Among the numerous short narrative prose forms that have appeared in the literature of the GDR, the *Erzählung,* emerging more and more as a notable genre in its own right, is the most popular.[28] In a review of Jurij Brězan's

---

[26]   *WB,* 16, No. 9 (1970), 97.

[27]   Eds. Ursula Steinhaußen, Dieter Faulseit, Jürgen Bonk (Berlin: Verlag Tribüne, 1969), p. 124.

[28]   The *Novelle,* though often mentioned together with the *Erzählung,* is not as common in the 60's and early 70's. See, for example, *Literaturkunde: Beiträge zu Wesen und Formen der Dichtung,* where it says that the "breiter ausmalende, verweilende Erzählung" takes precedence over the *Novelle.* It also says: "Nur ganz vereinzelt sind in den letzten Jahren Werke erschienen, denen der Autor die verpflichtende Genrebezeichnung Novelle gibt" (p. 164).

collection of *Erzählungen, Der Mäuseturm,*[29] the critic mentions the "Auf-
schwung, den die Kunst der Erzählung nach Umfang und Güte in unserer
gegenwärtigen Literatur erlebt . . ."[30] Arno Hochmuth observes: "In den
letzten Jahren wurden besonders Erzählungen bekannt . . ."[31]

The *Erzählung* is not easily defined; the *Handbuch für schreibende Arbeiter*
admits: "Die Erzählung ist als Genre nicht exakt definierbar, weil sie keine
strengen verbindlichen Formgesetze kennt. Sie steht zwischen Novelle und
Roman, und die Übergänge sind fließend."[32]

Some confusion has existed in the case of the longer *Erzählung* and the
short novel. For example, Christa Wolf's book *Der geteilte Himmel* has been
designated as an *Erzählung* in one edition, and as a novel in another.[33]
Similarly, Karl-Heinz Jakobs' *Beschreibung eines Sommers,*[34] with the subtitle
"Roman," is usually referred to as an *Erzählung* in critical discussions.[35]
According to Horst Simon in his article "Was Erzählungen Neues entdecken,"[36]
the *Erzählung* was sometimes looked upon as "eine Vorform" of a novel and as
"ein experimentelles Genre" (p. 4). But this view has been changing in recent
years, especially after 1965. Pracht and Neubert observe in *Sozialistischer
Realismus* (1970): "Erzählungen erheben nicht mehr den Anspruch, kleine
Romane zu sein; sie werden nicht nur als Vorform zur größeren epischen Form
verstanden" (p. 205). Thus, the *Erzählung* has become a genre in its own right.

This narrative prose form does not contain the manifold and varied
episodes of a novel, but rather takes one event and develops it fully. Its method
of narration, its loose structure and leisurely pace, its attention to detail,
remind one of a novel, but since the *Erzählung* has fewer characters and a single
plot, it moves within a more carefully delineated sphere. Thus, Horst Simon
observes in his article "Was Erzählungen Neues entdecken": "Ob in ihr eine
Handlung auf knappen fünf Seiten erzählt oder ein umfangreiches, verwickeltes
und beziehungsreiches Geschehen auf über 200 Seiten ausgebreitet wird, immer
bleibt der Horizont der Geschichte überschaubar" (p. 4).

The *Erzählung* often shows greater freedom in capturing and presenting
society than the novel, which builds up a complex world of its own in which its
characters move. Horst Simon observes that the possibilities of the *Erzählung*

[29]   Berlin: Verlag Neues Leben, 1970.
[30]   Hans-Jürgen Geisthardt, "Wahres und Wundersames," *NDL,* 19, No. 8 (1971), 132.
[31]   "Zum Problem der Massenwirksamkeit unserer Gegenwartsliteratur," *WB,* 17, No. 10
(1971), 10.
[32]   Steinhaußen et al., p. 132.
[33]   Cf. *Der geteilte Himmel: Erzählung* (Halle/Saale: Mitteldeutscher Verlag, 1963); *Der
geteilte Himmel: Roman* (Berlin-Schöneberg: Weiss, 1964).
[34]   Berlin: Verlag Neues Leben, 1962.
[35]   As, for example, by Eva Strittmatter, "Literatur und Wirklichkeit," in *Kritik in der
Zeit,* p. 510.
[36]   *Neues Deutschland,* 25 June 1972, p. 4.

are found above all in the fact that it can more directly and, at the same time, more quickly, react to the "jeweils neuen Momente in unserer Wirklichkeit . . . als dies dem Roman gegeben ist" (ibid.). In contrast to the *Kurzgeschichte* and *Novelle*, the *Erzählung*, too, has greater freedom; it is "freier, beweglicher, reicher an Handlung und an feinen Einzelheiten. . . . Abschweifungen, Einschübe, Kommentare sind ebenso möglich wie ausführliche Detailschilderungen . . ."[37] It does not have to limit itself to the conciseness and compression of the *Kurzgeschichte*, nor to the recounting of a unique or extraordinary event, which is the case of the *Novelle:* "Es kann durchaus eine sogenannte Alltagsbegebenheit sein, die der Autor aufgreift und durch die Art seines Erzählens, die nicht an strenge Formgesetze gebunden ist, lebendig werden läßt" (ibid.).

The *Erzählung* lends itself well to expressing and presenting the theme of the individual and society. This is particularly true because of the fact that it concentrates on one or two characters, and in this way an individual's interaction with society, with those around him, and with his collective, is brought out in sharp relief. Horst Simon observes in his article "Was Erzählungen Neues entdecken":

> Die Konzeption der ganzen Erzählhandlung derart, daß es hauptsächlich nur um die Ausprägung einer solchen Gestalt, ihrer charakterlichen Eigenart und ihrer Leistungen in Beruf, Familie und den von ihr eroberten Lebensbereichen geht, finden wir sehr häufig. (p. 4)

Thus, the *Erzählung* has become a popular genre for expressing and portraying the life of the individual in the new society in the literature of the GDR.

The emergence of the *Kurzgeschichte*

The *Kurzgeschichte* as a genre in its own right is a relatively recent phenomenon in the literature of the GDR. Whereas there have always been *Erzählungen* since the beginning of the new state, the first *Kurzgeschichte* appeared in 1967 with the publication of Manfred Jendryschik's *Glas und Ahorn*,[38] followed by Siegfried Pitschmann's "Der Direktor,"[39] and Bernd Jentzsch's "Josefski."[40] Although perhaps some of Johannes Bobrowski's

---

[37] *Hinweise für schreibende Arbeiter* (Leipzig: Verlag für Buch- und Bibliothekswesen, 1961), p. 58.

[38] Rostock: Hinstorff, 1967.

[39] In *Kontrapunkte: Geschichten und kurze Geschichten* (Berlin: Aufbau-Verlag, 1968).

[40] In *Neunzehn Erzähler der DDR*, ed. Hans-Jürgen Schmitt, Fischer Taschenbuch, 1210 (Frankfurt am Main: Fischer, 1971).

stories, written in the first half of the sixties, would also fall into the category of *Kurzgeschichte*, it was not consciously practised as a genre until after 1965, with the publication of the three above-mentioned works. This fact is an indication of a certain literary development in the GDR. In her essay "Laudatio auf die kleine Form," Renate Drenkow refers to a statement made by Erwin Strittmatter at a meeting of the *Deutscher Schriftstellerverband* in 1969: "Um Kurzgeschichten zu schreiben, bedarf es eines bestimmten Standes des Bewußtseins der Gesellschaft" (p. 96). She explains his remark in the following way:

> Er zielte dabei auf die Kurzgeschichte mit sozialistischer Gegenwartsthematik ... Die einzelnen 'kleinen' Geschichten ... sollen sozialistisches Bewußtsein befördern, sie verlangen jedoch auch einen Leser, der zur Assoziation in Blickrichtung Sozialismus fähig ist ... Im besonderen Maße gilt das für die sozialistisch-realistische Kurzgeschichte ... (pp. 96–97)

If the *Kurzgeschichte,* which depends on allusions and a kind of literary shorthand, wants to appeal to a large audience and to try to shape its consciousness, it requires readers who are well informed and acquainted with the problems of the emerging socialism presented in the *Kurzgeschichten.* Therefore some time had to pass after the founding of the GDR in 1949, before the genre could be used effectively. Manfred Jendryschik points out that the literary representation of a new society requires new forms and symbols, "die aber erst immer mehr präzisiert und so lebendig gemacht werden können, wie sich die Gesellschaft entwickelt ..."[41] Thus, during the early development of the socialist state, especially during the fifties, according to Jendryschik, "als sich die ideologische Umwälzung am gravierendsten vollzog" (ibid.), the chances of success in reaching a wide and receptive reading public were greater for the longer narrative forms with their descriptive and detailed presentation, than for the *Kurzgeschichte,* "die durch die genaue Zeichnung von Alltagsdetails lebt und in hohem Maße die Kenntnis, das Einverständnis, das Selbstbewußtsein, die politische Bildung des Lesenden braucht" (ibid.). Now the conditions for it have become favourable, and the existence and success of the *Kurzgeschichte* is even taken as an indication of the advanced stage of the socialist society in the GDR. Jendryschik concludes: "Der breite und bunte Fächer unserer Gegenwarts-Kurzgeschichte ist der Ausdruck einer entwickelten Gesellschaft ..." (ibid., p. 435).

There are diversities of opinion about its origin. Some critics, like Jendryschik, consider it to be a modern genre and refer to Hemingway and Babel as its chief influences (ibid., pp. 430–32). Other critics view it as being

---

[41] "Geschichten über Geschichten," in *Bettina pflückt wilde Narzissen: 66 Geschichten von 44 Autoren* (Halle/Saale: Mitteldeutscher Verlag, 1972), p. 430.

part of an older traditional form, the *Kalendergeschichte*. For example, Gerhard Rothbauer, writing about Joachim Nowotny's stories, observes: "Sein Ehrgeiz zielt nicht auf eine diffizile Assoziationskette . . . er erzählt viel eher in der Haltung eines Kalendergeschichten-Schreibers und ist damit durchaus in der legitimen Tradition der Kurzgeschichte."[42] Günter and Johanna Braun, on the other hand, define the *Kurzgeschichte* as a light and witty story: "Eine Kurzgeschichte ist eine kurze Geschichte, in deren Schlußpointe eine gesellschaftliche Erkenntnis blitzartig aufleuchtet . . ."[43] According to them, its purpose is mainly that of entertainment.

Probably each writer adjusts this literary form to suit his own purposes and temperament, and each critic relates the term to a different set of stories. Hence the difficulty of defining it. In the manual *Hinweise für schreibende Arbeiter* the following observation is made: "Die Kurzgeschichte . . . wurde erst im 20. Jahrhundert in Deutschland wirklich heimisch. Gleichwohl gibt es eine Unzahl von Spielarten dieses Genres, die eine genaue Definition erschweren" (p. 56). And Manfred Jendryschik regrets "Die Schwierigkeit, die Kurzgeschichte als literarische Form, als besondere Möglichkeit, als Struktur mit einzigartigen Gesetzen zu bestimmen . . ."[44] Many *Kurzgeschichten* could easily have been influenced by the *Kalendergeschichte,* because of its popular appeal (*Volkstümlichkeit*) and its pedagogical qualities. But the modern influence is probably strongest. In any case, it has been modified to fit into the mainstream of socialist realism. Thus Günter Jäckel uses the term "sozialistische Kurzgeschichte"[45] to describe it. "Es liegt im Wesen der Flexibilität dieses Genres, daß es nicht mit theoretischen Ansprüchen überlastet werden darf" (ibid., p. 143), he concludes.

Jäckel points to some of its qualities when he observes:

> Dem Bedürfnis des Lesers nach Informationsverdichtung Rechnung zu tragen, mit einem Minimum an Worten ein Höchstmaß an Aussage zu bringen und auch im 'Splitter' die 'neuen Grunderlebnisse' zu zeigen, Erinnerungen an den 'vergangenen Tag' zu überprüfen und damit offen zu sein für die Frage, wie man morgen leben soll, ist auch Anliegen dieses Genres. (ibid., pp. 137–38)

Brevity and conciseness and the ability to reveal a larger whole by portraying only one facet of it, are its characteristic qualities. At the same time, the "sozialistische Kurzgeschichte," as Jäckel calls it, also shows the same concern

---

[42] "Wie sich die 'verborgene Sache' beim Erzählen offenbart," *NDL,* 19, No. 8 (1971), 140.

[43] "Hundert Mark für eine Definition oder Ein Nachwort," in *Die Nase des Neandertalers: Kurzgeschichten* (Berlin: Verlag Neues Leben, 1969), p. 193.

[44] "Geschichten über Geschichten," p. 432.

[45] "Zwischen Erinnerungen und Vertrauen," *NDL,* 20, No. 1 (1972), 137.

for content and the representation of the new society, as do the other works of socialist realism.

Though the *Kurzgeschichte* is a more recent phenomenon in East German literature, it is becoming firmly established as a short narrative prose form in its own right. The significance and versatility of this genre in the literature of the GDR is suggested by Manfred Jendryschik:

> Heute zeigt sich die Kurzgeschichte in unserem Land als ein selbständiger Prosatyp, der eine erstaunliche Skala von der politisch agitatorischen bis zur psychologisch-seismographischen Variante mit allen Verflechtungen vorstellt, der mittelbar und unmittelbar die veränderten Erscheinungen unserer sozialistischen Gegenwart darstellt und durch die Darstellung in diese Gegenwart eingreift, um Veränderungen zu bewirken.[46]

Why the period since 1965 was chosen for this study

Beginning with the year 1965, the *Erzählung* became more popular than ever before, and at the same time the *Kurzgeschichte* became prominent. Whereas before 1965 only a limited number of collections of *Erzählungen* appeared, there has been a striking increase in the years following. For example, from 1960 to 1964 only five or six collections of *Erzählungen* were published, but in the single year 1971 more than double that number of anthologies and collections of both *Erzählungen* and *Kurzgeschichten* appeared.[47] This is a dramatic increase, and it indicates the popularity which these two narrative prose forms are now enjoying. In his recent article "Was Erzählungen Neues entdecken," Horst Simon observes:

---

[46] "Geschichten über Geschichten," p. 436.

[47] In 1960–64: e.g., Horst Boas, *Die Botschaft* (Berlin: Union Verlag, 1962); Günter de Bruyn, *Ein schwarzer, abgrundtiefer See* (Halle/Saale: Mitteldeutscher Verlag, 1963); Karl-Heinz Jakobs, *Merkwürdige Landschaften* (Halle/Saale: Mitteldeutscher Verlag, 1964); Erik Neutsch, *Bitterfelder Geschichten* (Halle/Saale: Mitteldeutscher Verlag, 1961); Horst Rühlicke, *Das elfte Jahr* (Berlin: Union Verlag, 1964). In 1971: e.g., Werner Bräunig, *Gewöhnliche Leute* (Halle/Saale: Mitteldeutscher Verlag, 1971); Helmut T. Heinrich, *Hölderlin auf dem Wege von Bordeaux* (Berlin: Aufbau-Verlag, 1971); Manfred Jendryschik, *Die Fackel und der Bart* (Rostock: Hinstorff, 1971); Harald Korall, ed., *Literatur 71: Almanach* (Halle/Saale: Mitteldeutscher Verlag, 1971); Hanna-Heide Kraze, *Steinchen schmeißen: Kindergeschichten für Erwachsene* (Berlin: Union Verlag, 1971); Günter Kunert, *Ortsangaben* (Berlin: Aufbau-Verlag, 1971); *Landung auf Paradies-Ort: Liebesgeschichten* (Berlin: Buchverlag Der Morgen, 1971); Helga Schütz, *Vorgeschichten oder Schöne Gegend Probstein* (Berlin: Aufbau-Verlag, 1971); *Die vierte Laterne: Voranmeldung*, eds. Joachim Schmidt et al. (Halle/Saale: Mitteldeutscher Verlag, 1971); Benito Wogatzki, *Der Preis des Mädchens* (Berlin: Verlag Neues Leben, 1971).

> In der letzten Zeit hat sich bei uns im Hinblick auf das epische Genre Erzählung eine
> neue Situation ergeben: Sie ist wieder zu einer normalen Erscheinung geworden und
> hat ihre Existenzberechtigung und Eigenständigkeit nunmehr wohl endgültig be-
> hauptet. ... Nicht daß der Roman nun weniger gefragt wäre oder erwartet würde.
> Erzählungen oder sogar Erzählungsbände gibt es inzwischen in einer so großen Zahl,
> daß es nicht schwerfällt, nur aus den letzten zwei, drei Jahren ... an die zwanzig
> Erzählbände zusammenzustellen. (p. 4)

Another reason why the *Erzählung* and *Kurzgeschichte* written after 1965 have been chosen for this study is the fact that the theme of the individual and the new society became more and more prominent after that date, as part of a general trend which can be observed in the literature of the GDR. In the fifties, themes from the immediate past, as, for example, the war, concentration camps, fascism, the resistance movement, captivity, and exile were depicted. Franz Fühmann, in his *Novelle Kameraden* (1955) and his *Erzählung* "Kapitulation" (1957), portrays the inhumanity of fascist armies. Novels like *Die Patrioten* (1954) by Bodo Uhse, *Nackt unter Wölfen* (1958) by Bruno Apitz, and *Die Fahne von Kriwoj Rog* (1959) by Otto Gotsche, tell the story of the anti-fascist resistance fighters. Many novels and *Erzählungen* deal with the theme of the young man who gains insight after having been misled by fascism, as, for example, the *Erzählungen Der Mann und sein Name* (1952) by Anna Seghers and *Bis zum letzten Mann* (1957) by Karl Mundstock, and the novels *Die Lüge* (1956) by Herbert Otto, *Der Gymnasiast* (1958) and *Semester der verlorenen Zeit* (1960) by Jurij Brězan, and *Die Abenteuer des Werner Holt* (1960) by Dieter Noll. Other works deal with the part played by communists in the Weimar Republic and under Hitler, and with their new role in the reconstruction of a socialist Germany; *Ein neues Kapitel* (1959) by Hans Marchwitza, and *Die Entscheidung* (1959) by Anna Seghers are some examples.

Other works of narrative fiction concern themselves with economic production, as, for example, *Roheisen* (1955) by Hans Marchwitza, or with socialist changes in rural life, as, for example, *Der Weg über den Acker* (1955) by Margarete Neumann. These works deal mainly with the early beginnings of socialist society in the GDR. After the First Bitterfeld Conference in 1959 writers began to turn their attention primarily to the portrayal of the worker and his relationships in a socialist society. Many writers accepted the invitation extended by the Conference to work in an industrial plant and later wrote about their experiences. For example, Brigitte Reimann went to the *Braun-kohlekombinat* "Schwarze Pumpe" and wrote the *Erzählung Ankunft im Alltag* (1961); Christa Wolf also went to work in a manufacturing plant and wrote the best known *Brigadegeschichte, Der geteilte Himmel* (1963). Erik Neutsch, too, gained first-hand working experience in a brigade and wrote a collection of shorter *Erzählungen* called *Bitterfelder Geschichten* (1961), which were inspired by the ideals set forth by the Conference.

The literature of the early sixties reflects the economic development of the GDR; the individual is shown actively engaged in reconstruction and building, the establishing of LPG's, and in adapting to new ways of thinking. Klaus Jarmatz observes:

> Seit der ersten Bitterfelder Konferenz hatten viele Schriftsteller erhebliche Anstrengungen darauf gerichtet, sich enger mit dem neuen gesellschaftlichen Leben zu verbinden und der neuen Wirklichkeit auch literarisch auf den Fersen zu bleiben.[48]

This trend becomes more and more evident in the sixties, as the worker, actively involved in socialist society, comes more and more to the fore as a literary figure. Hans Jürgen Geerdts points out in his introduction to *Literatur in der DDR in Einzeldarstellungen*[49] that the portrayal of the interaction between the individual and society appears frequently in the literature of the past decade (p. XXI). Klaus Jarmatz also mentions the fact that in the second half of the sixties the "*bewußte* Gestaltung einer neuen Gesellschaft, die Freisetzung menschlicher Möglichkeiten,"[50] becomes the main theme of contemporary literature in the GDR. Thus, it is particularly the literature written after 1965 that is well suited for a study of the theme of the individual in a new society.

The objectives of this study

This study will attempt to investigate the presentation and portrayal of the individual in a new society in a number of selected *Erzählungen* and *Kurzgeschichten* written in the GDR between 1965 and 1972. These two popular short narrative prose forms, which limit themselves to one or two main characters and one event or action, are eminently suited to express and illuminate some facets of the individual's relationship to his society as seen by writers who live within the socialist society. However, in spite of their increasing importance, which has often been stressed by East German critics, and their growing popularity, the fact remains that very little indeed has been done so far in studying this aspect of the literary production of the GDR. In her article "Laudatio auf die kleine Form," Renate Drenkow observes that the short narrative prose forms, in spite of their obvious importance, have been greatly neglected in literary discussions and that critical studies and investigations hardly exist (p. 95). She concludes:

---

[48]   "Kritik in der Zeit," in *Kritik in der Zeit*, p. 66.
[49]   *Literatur der DDR in Einzeldarstellungen,* ed. H. J. Geerdts, Kröners Taschenausgabe, 416 (Stuttgart: Kröner, 1972).
[50]   "Kritik in der Zeit," p. 72.

Die Aufgabe steht noch bevor, anhand des reichen Materials in Anthologien und Erzählungsbänden den Anteil der kleinen Form bei der Bewältigung unserer Wirklichkeit zu bewerten und die in ihnen enthaltenen neuen Fragen gründlich zu diskutieren. (ibid.)

Even within the GDR, only one dissertation has so far been devoted to the study of the *Erzählung,* and it is limited to the period 1956 to 1963. It is a dissertation by Sigrid Bock, "Probleme des Menschenbildes in Erzählungen und Novellen (Beitrag zur Geschichte der sozialistisch-realistischen Erzählkunst in der DDR von 1956/57 bis 1963)."[51] The histories of literature, as, for example, Konrad Franke, *Die Literatur der Deutschen Demokratischen Republik,*[52] and Fritz J. Raddatz, *Traditionen und Tendenzen: Materialien zur Literatur der DDR,*[53] are general and superficial in their discussion of the short prose forms. Theodore Huebener's *The Literature of East Germany*[54] is a rather general introduction to individual authors, and *Literatur der DDR in Einzeldarstellungen,* edited by Hans Jürgen Geerdts, though it discusses briefly some *Erzählungen,* consists of monographs on various writers. The most pertinent and useful material is that found scattered in the introductions to various anthologies of *Erzählungen* and *Kurzgeschichten,* and in a number of articles and reviews.

The aim of this investigation is to examine recurring themes, motifs, and literary types found in a number of representative *Erzählungen* and *Kurzgeschichten,* and to discover the common concerns and intentions of the writers. In what way is the individual presented in his relationship to his work, his collective, and the other aspects of socialist society in these narrative prose works? In considering this question, literary form itself recedes into the background, which is in keeping with the attitude of most writers of the GDR, who consider form to be of secondary importance.

Representative writers of *Erzählungen* like Werner Bräunig, Manfred Jendryschik, Erik Neutsch, Joachim Nowotny, and Siegfried Pitschmann have been chosen for this study, as well as individual *Erzählungen* and *Kurzgeschichten* in the work of Volker Braun, Werner Heiduczek, Erwin Strittmatter, Benito Wogatzki and a number of other writers of the GDR. The stories of the "writing-workers" (*schreibende Arbeiter*) contained in numerous anthologies[55] have been omitted, because as amateur prose writers they are in a different category and deserve a separate study.

---

[51]   Diss. Institut für Gesellschaftswissenschaften beim ZK der SED, Berlin, 1964.
[52]   München: Kindler, 1971.
[53]   Frankfurt am Main: Suhrkamp, 1972.
[54]   New York: Ungar, 1970.
[55]   See, for example, *Bitterfelder Ernte: Eine Anthologie schreibender Arbeiter des Bezirkes Halle, 1959–1967,* ed. Bezirksvorstand des FGDB Halle und der Rat des Bezirkes Halle (Berlin: Verlag Tribüne, 1968); *Der Tag hat 24 Stunden: Eine Anthologie des Zirkels*

Besides the lack of emphasis on literary form, a peculiarity of East German literature as a whole, another limitation should be kept in mind. There is a pronounced unanimity of opinion on the printed word in the GDR and the writers are a highly homogeneous group; therefore, a theoretical statement made by one individual writer or critic may usually be taken as being representative of the majority of them. Hence, it is usually possible to quote such a statement made by an author without defining his viewpoint, for it can be assumed that it reflects the collective awareness of Marxist writers and literary theoreticians. For the same reason, it would not be helpful for this study to compare one East German critic with another, or to make any kind of evaluative statement about the merits of any one critic. On the other hand, it is possible to use the pronouncements of one writer or critic, as has been done in this study, to clarify and comment on the purpose and intention of another writer's work.

The findings have been grouped into six chapters, each of which emphasizes one facet of the relationship of the individual in a socialist society as shown in various *Erzählungen* and *Kurzgeschichten.* The first three chapters concentrate on three themes or motifs: the role of work, the collective, and the theme of social change in the life of the individual in the new society. Chapters IV to VI centre around three groups of individuals commonly portrayed in the literature of the GDR: the emancipated woman, the outsider, and the "positive" hero. I consider these to be the main aspects of the theme of the individual in socialist society as revealed in *Erzählungen* and *Kurzgeschichten* of the GDR written after 1965.

schreibender Arbeiter im VEB Petrolchemisches Kombinat Schwedt (Berlin: Verlag Tribüne, 1971); *Verflixte Gedanken: Prosa schreibender Arbeiter,* eds. Hans Schmidt, Wolfgang Himmelreich, Anita Baldauf (Berlin: Verlag Tribüne, 1970).

A. Themes and Directions

Chapter I
THE ROLE OF WORK

The theme of work plays a significant role in the literature of the GDR; again and again it appears in the *Erzählungen* and *Kurzgeschichten* that portray the new society. In socialist realism, as Elisabeth Simons observes, literary figures are presented in terms of their relationship to the working world: "Alle markanten literarischen Prosa-Gestalten sind im Bezug zu ihrer Arbeitssphäre erfaßt. Das kennzeichnet die Figurenzeichnung des sozialistischen Realismus."[1] When a writer of the GDR depicts the every-day problems and relationships of the individual in the sphere of work, his literary productions are meaningful and topical. Hella Dietz in "Die Rede geht von uns," her review of Erik Neutsch's stories *Die anderen und ich,*[2] remarks:

> Was der Schriftsteller in seinem jüngsten Buch des Erzählens für wert hält, sind Fragen nach der besonderen sozialistischen Qualität zwischenmenschlicher Beziehungen in der wichtigsten Lebenssphäre des Menschen, in der Arbeit. Neutsch fragt nach den *heutigen* Problemen in diesen Beziehungen, er fragt nach den *heutigen* Problemen in der Arbeit.[3]

In dealing with the theme of work, the socialist writer can help the reader to see himself more clearly and thus enable him to understand his problems and his duty to society better. Pracht and Neubert make the following observation: "Durch die Darstellung von Arbeitergestalten in der Kunst wird es möglich, die Lebensprobleme von Menschen zu erfassen, die sich in der Arbeit ihrer neuen Aufgaben bewußt werden und ihre Persönlichkeit entwickeln ..." (pp. 172–73).

Moreover, according to Anna Seghers, the individual can only be portrayed truly in terms of his work; she said in her lecture "Die Tiefe und Breite in der Literatur" (1960)[4] : "Heute und hier, in der Arbeit und durch die Arbeit, wird der Mensch erst völlig kenntlich" (p. 490), and "Sein Charakter wird klar in seinem Verhältnis zur Arbeit. An den Besonderheiten der Arbeit erkennt man die Besonderheiten des Charakters. In der Wirklichkeit und in der Darstellung" (p. 491).

But the main reason for the central place given to work in the literature of the GDR is simply the "Lebenstatsache" (p. 172), as Pracht and Neubert call it,

---

[1] " 'Das Andersmachen, von Grund Auf': Die Hauptrichtung der jüngsten erzählenden DDR-Literatur," *WB,* 15, Sonderheft (1969), 197.
[2] Halle/Saale: Mitteldeutscher Verlag, 1970.
[3] "Die Rede geht von uns," *NDL,* 19, No. 2 (1971), 177.
[4] In *Kritik in der Zeit.*

that "neue Wesenszüge sozialistischer Persönlichkeiten . . . sich zuerst in der Arbeiterklasse [entwickeln]" (ibid.). Thus, according to socialist doctrine, the labourer, the member of the working class, is the man with the most correct and progressive views. The new man of socialism is developed by labour, and art has to learn from him and portray him.

Work and the development of the socialist personality

"Junge Schriftsteller unserer Republik haben in den letzten Jahren vor allem darum gerungen, die Formung der Menschen durch die sozialistische Arbeit künstlerisch zu gestalten,"[5] observes Helga Herting. Volker Braun has depicted this in his *Erzählung Das ungezwungne Leben Kasts,*[6] in which the young hero is changed as he digs ditches and lays pipes together with the other members of the work brigade. At the beginning of the story, he confesses: "Ich war völlig leer, gleichgültig; ich sah alles an wie eine fremde, unbekannte Gegend" (p. 9). But later, after he has been transformed by his experience of collective work, he declares:

> Ich hatte noch nie eine solche Beziehung zu den Dingen um mich gehabt, früher hatte ich in den Einbildungen gelebt, die ich auf dem Papier erfand, jetzt floß eine große vollgefüllte Landschaft um mich, die sich vor den Händen bewegte, langsam, doch unaufhörlich, mit immer gleichen Bildern, doch sich zu etwas anderem ausbildend, das ich schon sah hinter dem Schlamm. (p. 33)

The change in Kast's attitude to the world around him is dramatic. It is like a rebirth for him. Throughout the *Erzählung,* Braun shows his hero's development as work gains a more and more central place in his life. Kast observes: "Die Arbeit, mit vielen und für viele, war alles aus dem ich was werden konnte, mich entwickeln konnte" (p. 25).

The heroes of Werner Bräunig's *Erzählungen,* as, for example, "Gewöhnliche Leute,"[7] are completely involved in the life of the new society and already reveal well-developed socialist personalities. Nevertheless, Hannes Stütz and Adele Noth are shown developing even further as their talents and enthusiasm are daily challenged by the tasks around them. Hannes realizes his full potential and that of his work crew when he makes the daring decision — and succeeds in it — of racing against time in order to finish the construction of a high-rise apartment a hundred and twenty days ahead of schedule. Thus, two

---

[5] *Das sozialistische Menschenbild in der Gegenwartsliteratur: Beiträge zur Kunsterziehung* (Berlin: Verlag Tribüne, 1966), p. 17.

[6] Edition Neue Texte (Berlin: Aufbau-Verlag, 1972).

[7] In *Gewöhnliche Leute* (Halle/Saale: Mitteldeutscher Verlag, 1971).

individuals, Hannes and Adele, find themselves and each other as they work together in the new society, represented in this case by the construction site. They make important decisions about their lives, thus asserting their individuality, and they realize their true potential in their work. Hermann Scheler observes:

> Vor allem und gerade in der Sphäre der sozialistischen Produktion entwickelt die neue Persönlichkeit ihre reiche Individualität, ihre schöpferischen Fähigkeiten und Talente, vollbringt sie die neuen Heldentaten der Arbeit und des Werktagslebens.[8]

The *Erzählung* "Kraftstrom"[9] by Erwin Strittmatter shows how Old Adam, who appears to be relegated to a useless existence, "ein gelbes Herbstblatt" (p. 128), is given a new lease of life through work. Unexpectedly a new world opens up to him as he services the electric fence that guards the cattle herd and as he marvels over the wonders of electricity. Thus, even in his old age, he is again able to grow and develop, as the narrow limits of his horizon are broken through by work in the new society. The story ends with the line: "Der alte Adam ist mächtig am Leben" (p. 132).

The important decision that led to Old Adam's rejuvenation and renewed vigour was made in the area of work. Similarly, Hannes and Adele develop as socialist personalities in the midst of their work on the construction site, and Kast is transformed through work. Whether young or old, the individuals in these *Erzählungen* are helped to develop socialist personalities and find meaning in their lives by means of work.

Work and morality

Closely related to the role of work in creating the socialist personality is its function in the development of a new socialist morality. "Aus der neuen Stellung der Arbeit und des arbeitenden Menschen ergeben sich neue moralische Triebkräfte,"[10] observes Erhard John. Work in the new society is a force which strengthens moral fibre. Those who are outside of its discipline and challenge are decadent and self-centred. An example of this is Gerhard Koblenz, the son of the chief architect in Erik Neutsch's *Erzählung* "Drei Tage

---

[8] "Die Dialektik von gesellschaftlichem Gesamtwillen und Einzelwillen der sozialistischen Persönlichkeit," *Deutsche Zeitschrift für Philosophie*, 16, No. 10 (1968), 1175.

[9] In *Ein Dienstag im September: 16 Romane im Stenogramm* (Berlin: Aufbau-Verlag, 1969).

[10] "Sozialistisches Menschenbild und humanistische Traditionen," in *Das Sozialistische Menschenbild: Weg und Wirklichkeit*, eds. Elmar Faber and Erhard John, 2nd ed. (Leipzig: Karl-Marx-Universität, 1968), p. 43.

unseres Lebens."[11] He cheats in school, rides around on his motorcycle, plays jazz and rock and roll in a cellar, and has no morals, having seduced Sigrid Seidensticker, the daughter of a streetcar operator. Sigrid's father tells the mayor, the narrator of the story, how his widowed mother had raised her large family "in Anstand" (p. 176), and the mayor thinks: "Ja, eine solche Moral täte einem Jungen wie Gerhard Koblenz ganz gut. Er müßte mal wissen, daß das Leben auch Pflichten enthält" (ibid.). Since he is not working and has no responsibilities, he is portrayed as an idler, whose life-style and lack of morals go together.

In the *Erzählung* "Ein Tag und eine Nacht"[12] by Benito Wogatzki, the hero remarks about Ursula, the wife of a truckdriver in his work brigade, that she should be given some demanding work. This would prevent her from seeking diversion in dance halls and extra-marital affairs, and provide her with a suitable challenge:

> Die wußte ja schon wieder nicht ... wohin mit der Unrast, wohin eigentlich mit der drängenden, quälenden Kraft ihrer zwanzig Jahre. Sie brauchte so etwas wie einen Bagger in die Hände — einen versackten, wenn es geht —, eine Tafel voll Formeln, einen brüllenden Meister, irgendeine furchtbar schwere Angelegenheit ... (p. 400)

The author implies that because she has never learned to work properly and to have a responsible position, her moral sense has not been developed. Work would strengthen her moral fibre.

The morality that is developed through work in the new society is largely an *Arbeitsmoral,* as it is called. The one who possesses it is an exemplary worker with a socialist personality. In his *Erzählung* "Akte Nora S.,"[13] Erik Neutsch portrays such an individual. A dedicated and ambitious worker, Nora is eager to make new discoveries, not for her own selfish advancement, but for the sake of socialist society. She even takes personal hardship upon herself for the sake of accomplishing her task successfully. Thus she has a true *Arbeitsmoral.* Erhard John observes: "Tatsächlich ist das Herausbilden einer hohen Arbeitsmoral eines der wichtigsten Elemente der sozialistischen Persönlichkeitsbildung."[14]

The main emphasis in the *Erzählungen* is on the *Arbeitsmoral* of an individual, a quality always associated with the socialist worker. The individual's private life and his moral standards are based on it. Thus, characters like Ursula in Wogatzki's "Ein Tag und eine Nacht" and Gerhard Koblenz in

---

[11] In *Die anderen und ich* (Halle/Saale: Mitteldeutscher Verlag, 1970).
[12] In *Manuskripte: Almanach neuer Prosa und Lyrik,* eds. Joachim Ret, Achim Roscher, Heinz Sachs (Halle/Saale: Mitteldeutscher Verlag, 1969).
[13] In *Die anderen und ich.*
[14] "Sozialistisches Menschenbild und humanistische Traditionen," p. 44.

Neutsch's "Drei Tage unseres Lebens," who are not working, do not possess a socialist personality and an *Arbeitsmoral,* and, at the same time, they also lack moral standards in their private lives.

Work in socialist society also develops a new ethical viewpoint in personal relationships and attitudes to others. In the *Erzählung* "Der Preis des Mädchens"[15] by Benito Wogatzki, the protagonist, a young executive sent to improve production in an affiliated industrial plant, falls in love with a girl working on one of the assembly lines. She has an illegitimate child, but she is a fine worker with a socialist personality. He overcomes his bourgeois prejudice and decides to marry her. Thus he learns not to judge superficially or by conventional standards, but from a new ethical standpoint. In his essay "Unsere Konflikte in unserer Literatur," Werner Neubert makes the following observation:

> Von hier aus — von der sozialistischen Arbeit als dem *Kernstück* der neuen menschlichen Beziehungen ... leiten sich primär alle Konflikte und Probleme der gesellschaftlichen Vorwärtsbewegung ab: das Verhältnis zwischen Mann und Frau, die Probleme von Liebe und Ehe, das Streben des Individuums nach Glück ... das Werden einer neuen Moral und Ethik.[16]

The individual's ethical viewpoint and his attitude and sense of responsibility to others in his private relationships are changed by work in the new society.

Work as the creator of man

From what has been said already, it can be seen that socialism emphasizes labour as a shaping and moral force in man. According to its tenets, not only does man produce or create something by means of his work, he is himself shaped by it. Man as an intelligent and social being is seen as having evolved in the process of countless centuries of labour as he tried to cope with his environment. In his treatise *Anteil der Arbeit an der Menschwerdung des Affen,* Friedrich Engels states:

> Die Arbeit ist die Quelle allen Reichtums, sagen die politischen Ökonomen. Sie ist dies ... Aber sie ist noch unendlich mehr als dies. Sie ist die erste Grundbedingung alles menschlichen Lebens, und zwar in einem solchen Grade, daß wir in gewissem Sinn sagen müssen: Sie hat den Menschen selbst geschaffen.[17]

---

[15] In *Der Preis des Mädchens.*
[16] "Unsere Konflikte in unserer Literatur," *NDL,* 18, No. 1 (1970), 9.
[17] (Berlin: Dietz, 1970), p. 6

Thus, in socialism labour is looked upon in a certain sense, according to Engels, as a force that creates man, and it is, therefore, vital in the life of the individual and society, for it stands at the centre of his life and relationships. In his essay "Persönlichkeit und Gemeinschaft in der sozialistischen Gesellschaft,"[18] Günter Heyden observes: "Man darf nicht vergessen, daß der Mensch durch die Arbeit zum Menschen geworden ist, daß er nur durch diese existiert" (p. 18). He also states: "Was die Menschen sind, sind sie durch ihre Arbeit. . . . Die besondere Existenzweise des Menschen ist durch sie bedingt und entwickelt sich auch mit ihr auf höherer Stufenleiter" (p. 10).

The central role of work in socialist thought is reflected in the literature of the GDR. The stories portray the relationships of the individual in the new society in terms of his relationship to work: by means of work he is changed and transformed, his socialist personality is allowed to develop, his true potential is tapped, and his life enriched and ennobled. Moreover, through his work, the individual discovers a new sense of unity and rapport with other members of his society.

Work integrates the isolated individual

One of the roles of work as it is presented in a number of stories is to act as an integrating force for the isolated individual, who at first finds himself outside the new society. In the *Erzählung Das ungezwungne Leben Kasts* by Volker Braun, physical labour is presented as the integrating force for the young hero. At the beginning of the story, Kast is immature, isolated and rebellious. He is a young man whose ideals about the new society have been shattered, for he has been expelled from school for expressing critical opinions about his society. Dissatisfied with himself and his world, and at a loss what to do with himself, he finally joins a work brigade which does manual labour. At first he is disappointed by the work, digging in the mud for weeks and months. He has a different idea of what building up socialism means; this seems backward and inefficient to him. He questions the purpose of his life: "Mein *Leben*, das ich beginnen wollte, wie mußte es sein? Es ging hin . . ." (p. 25). However, through his work he slowly finds himself and his place as a part of many; he becomes integrated into an organic and vital whole. This is highlighted in a dramatic event in the *Erzählung.* Severe flooding from a stream threatens to destroy a section of their construction. At night the labourers gather to save it, working to the utmost of their strength. The extremely difficult and arduous task brings them together and he becomes a part of the group:

[18] "Persönlichkeit und Gemeinschaft in der sozialistischen Gesellschaft," *Deutsche Zeitschrift für Philosophie*, 16, No. 1 (1968).

Ich sah die hellen Gestalten hinter den blendenden Lampen, bunt, nah, in Bewegung, sie arbeiteten im Graben, während ich müde hier stand. ... ich fühlte plötzlich das Verlangen, dort hinabzusteigen und die Müdigkeit abzuschütteln ... und ein Bestandteil dieses Bilds zu werden, und es mit zu füllen und zu bewegen. Ich floh von der Brücke herab. (pp. 45–46)

The picture of the labourers in the light of the floodlights, the harmony and the unity which it expresses, as well as the self-sacrifice of the workers and their willingness to take hardship upon themselves, impress him so much that he cannot but join them. In another part of the *Erzählung,* this experience is reinforced in Kast's life, when, as a student, he helps on an LPG at harvest time, and again experiences the unity and oneness with the farmers and other students as they work together. In both scenes depicted by the author, the moment of utmost integration of the individual with his fellow workers is stressed as a central and momentous event. The individual is full of his experience, which is based on feeling, rather than conscious awareness. As a result of it, the young loner is transformed, becoming an integrated member of the new society.

The *Erzählung* "Stillegung"[19] by Werner Bräunig offers a contrast to the one by Volker Braun in that Urban, the hero, is a seventy-year-old pensioner, who feels painfully his exclusion from the new society because he is not contributing to it anymore, and who seeks to be integrated into it again in order to find meaning in life. Consequently, he decides to go back to work to become a nightwatchman at a construction site in a new town being built.

The two worlds between which Urban chooses are contrasted: the old familiar one with his generations-old home and the past it represents, the other pensioners, who sit on benches and recall their memories, and, on the other hand, the new society, the bustling life of the workers, their talk of the latest happenings at the factory, which Urban hears and for which he envies them, and his room in a modern high-rise apartment as he takes up his work. When he has made his decision and arrives at the construction site, his place of work, he realizes with satisfaction that from that very moment he belongs to it. "Nachtwächter, das ist gerade nichts Umwerfendes, aber das ist nicht das Problem," he thinks. "Es gibt eben Dinge, die man noch vollbringen kann. Und das ist die Hauptsache" (p. 184).

Through his work Urban is integrated into the new society. The old world is quickly discarded because it is of no value, the new one counts above all else. What is admired, according to Werner Bräunig's *Erzählung,* is Urban's ability to change even at his age and to leave the past behind him, to look ahead and work for the future. But how he will be able to keep this up at his age, or what

[19] In *Gewöhnliche Leute.*

his resources, aside from his progressive socialist outlook, will be, are questions that are not being asked.

In the two *Erzählungen* "Gewöhnliche Leute" and "Der schöne Monat August"[20] by Werner Bräunig, the process of integration through work and the oneness of the individual and the new society are also portrayed and emphasized as essential experiences. These narratives present individuals who have found their role in society through their work; the heroes, Hannes Stütz and Peter Trumm, are happy and confident, because they are perfectly integrated with their world and society.

All the stories mentioned have this in common: they suggest that the individual who is isolated for whatever reason, finds his way into society through work. If he is without work, his relationship with society is broken; he is of no value.

In Erik Neutsch's *Erzählung* "Akte Nora S.," the integrating force of work is not able to operate in the heroine's life, because Färber and Likendeel, the two men who are her superiors at her place of work and also her lovers, are still caught up in the backward attitudes of bourgeois society and do not understand Nora, who is a progressive member of socialist society. They are selfish and self-centred and do not encourage her in her striving. Similarly, the firm which employs her considers only its own immediate requirements and fires her when her attitude proves to be an inconvenience to them, although Nora is a faithful worker and thinks of the greater good of the country. Thus work integrates the individual only with socialist society; if the individual is the progressive one, and those around him backward, it only serves to aggravate the rift.

Work unites individuals in the new society

Besides enabling the isolated individual to find his place in socialist society, work is also the uniting factor within the society itself. This is shown, for example, in Werner Bräunig's *Erzählung* "Gewöhnliche Leute," which portrays a busy construction site, a microcosm of the new society, knit together by activity and work. The relationships among the individuals are harmonious. The workers interact and devote their energy to building something together. They are part of an ideal world in which the individual and society have already become one, brought together by their work.

In this *Erzählung* by Bräunig, the meeting of Hannes Stütz and Adele Noth, the main characters, and much of their courting, take place at the construction site. Adele, who is a newcomer to the site, quickly feels at home in her new

[20] In *Gewöhnliche Leute*.

surroundings. Hannes thinks: "Sie gehörte nun dazu, und sie war selber wichtig genug. Sie ging neben ihm, und sie waren nun alte Bekannte. So, wie es war, war es gut" (p. 19). They have a sense of belonging to their sphere of work, of feeling at ease in it, and thus with each other; they are already "alte Bekannte." The words, "So, wie es war, war es gut," suggest their sense of emotional security.

Personal relationships gain a new quality in socialist society, because the individuals are self-confident, securely rooted in their society through their work and united by a common cause. Thus, love affairs, for example, work out smoothly as a result of the happy adjustment of both individuals to their work. The relationship of Hannes Stütz and Adele is harmonious from the time they meet, because of their sense of community, of being a part of it together. Conversely, their love enables them to contribute more intensely to their work. When they return to the construction site after an idyllic summer week-end, Werner Bräunig indicates their feeling of oneness with their work: "Sie kehrten zurück in den Rhythmus der Baustelle, der nahm sie auf . . ." (p. 50). But whereas Adele and Hannes are happy in their relationship together and it works out well, because they share the same work experience, Nora's affair with Färber, and later the one with Likendeel, in Erik Neutsch's story "Akte Nora S.," do not, since her world of work is out of harmony with the attitude of those around her; she has to sacrifice her love because it hinders her in accomplishing her work.

In Werner Bräunig's *Erzählung* "Die einfachste Sache der Welt,"[21] the title itself suggests that the relationship of the two main characters, a man and a woman, is uncomplicated and matter-of-fact. They meet at a lake, where the hero is enjoying his holidays, and they fall in love. It is a happy relationship, because of the security and confidence in themselves as persons given to them by their work and what it means to them.

Futhermore, even their enjoyment of their holidays is deeper because of the knowledge of their work in the background. Heinz Plavius observes: "Die Diskussion um eine Freizeit ohne den sinnerfüllenden Hintergrund der Arbeit heißt folglich, leeres Stroh dreschen."[22] Thus, an individual's work affects every aspect of his life, including his personal relationships and his leisure time.

Work in the new society also helps to remove any social differences between groups due to education or position. In Volker Braun's *Erzählung Das ungezwungne Leben Kasts,* the hero and his fellow students, who are helping at an LPG at harvest time, get to know the farmers by name, and there is active social interaction between them. Kast observes: "Wir kannten fast alle Bauern beim Namen . . . wir waren auch fester zu einer Gemeinschaft zusammen-

---

[21] In *Gewöhnliche Leute.*
[22] "Der positive Held im sozialistischen Realismus und der neue Charakter der Arbeit," *Deutsche Zeitschrift für Philosophie,* 11, No. 8 (1963), 942.

gewachsen. Und ich fühlte wieder deutlich, daß uns in dem Land wenig trennte und schon gar nicht Standesschranken . . ." (p. 78). In Helmut Sakowski's story "Wie sich das Nachdenken ausgezahlt hat,"[23] Elli-Marie, an agricultural specialist at an LPG, is loath to admit that her father is a scientist and professor, because it might create barriers between her and the farmers. The author comments: "Und wir wollen es [i.e., her family background] auch nur erwähnen, weil es deutlich macht, daß sich Menschen unterschiedlichster Bildung und Herkunft in den Dörfern um Dedelow zu gemeinsamer Arbeit zusammengefunden haben" (p. 204). Thus, in the new society any class differences are broken down in working together, or they simply become irrelevant.

Moreover, the common experience of work enables an individual to see his fellows with greater appreciation and insight. After toiling for many hours side by side with the other members of his work gang, Braun's hero in *Das ungezwungne Leben Kasts* suddenly sees them in a new light:

> Da saßen wir, naß und voll Dreck, hungrig auf Schlaf, die Muskeln wie zerschlagen. . . . Ich hatte nie so wie heut gesehn, was es für Menschen waren, die hier fern von ihren Familien und ihren Wohnungen, auf die Baustellen verstreut, im Land lagen. (p. 44)

Kast's general attitude towards others changes through the experience of working together; he learns to appreciate and respect them more.

Work as an aesthetic experience

In some *Erzählungen* comments are found about the beauty of work. Benito Wogatzki, in his *Erzählung* "Ein Tag und eine Nacht," declares: "Sinnvolle Arbeit, gute Arbeit, schöne Arbeit – das ist es, was bleibt" (p. 375). In *Das ungezwungne Leben Kasts,* Volker Braun's hero praises the beauty and hardness of work. In his first experience of back-breaking labour under difficult conditions requiring self-sacrifice, Kast observes: "Es war ein schönes eigenartiges Bild, ich sah jetzt, daß diese Arbeit eine Schönheit hatte . . ." (p. 46), and he is fascinated by it. Later, when he helps at an LPG at harvest time, he experiences the scene of people working together as a beautiful picture before him; he even sketches it: "Ich zeichnete die Gruppe bei der Arbeit, schaufelnd im Morast, Arme und Gesichter dreckig, unter der sengenden Sonne" (p. 78). The scenes of the people at work become for him aesthetic experiences.

Thus work becomes an aesthetic experience for Braun's hero. In connection with this, it should be noted that the type of work which left an impact on Kast's life and character and gripped his imagination is physical labour; the

---

[23]   In *Zwei Zentner Leichtigkeit: Geschichten* (Berlin: Verlag Neues Leben, 1971).

scenes associated with his aesthetic experience are those involving hard work
and hardship. They also suggest the total involvement of each individual; thus
the aesthetic appeal comes from the labour which is done together, a fact
which again points to the unifying force of work in socialist society.

The central role of work in the individual's life

Karl Marx, in his "Kritik des Gothaer Programms," speaks of the time when
"die Arbeit nicht nur Mittel zum Leben, sondern selbst das erste Lebensbedürfnis geworden [ist] . . ."[24] Thus, in socialism even man's relationship to
work itself undergoes an evolution. The significance of work to man is to grow
until it becomes the most important aspect of his life.

In Volker Braun's *Erzählung Das ungezwungne Leben Kasts,* the hero
undergoes a gradual development in which work becomes what may be called
"das erste Lebensbedürfnis." After he has become integrated with the new
society through the labour in which he takes part, he gradually learns to regard
work as the most important activity and goal in his life. At the end of the
Erzählung, when he and Susanne have the choice of staying together or of
living in two different cities so that both can follow their respective work, they
choose the latter, and only meet when they can. "Wir hatten uns entschieden.
Wir würden die Härte auf uns nehmen" (p. 140), says Kast. Thus, it is only in
the sphere of work that he is prepared to make his lasting commitments; in his
personal relationships, as, for example, his love affair with Linde, who loves
him and would like to marry him, he refuses to tie himself down. Kast is
portrayed as a progressive hero of socialism, who seeks to develop himself and
to find the meaning of life in his work. Echoing Karl Marx, Heinz Plavius
observes:

Das Bild des kommunistischen Menschen wird von seinem Verhältnis zur Arbeit
bestimmt. Die Arbeit verwandelt sich aus einer Last in das erste Lebensbedürfnis. Der
Held des sozialistisch-realistischen Kunstwerks kann also nur lebensfähig sein, wenn
seine Züge von diesem Grundgesetz seines Lebens bestimmt werden.[25]

Similarly, in Erik Neutsch's "Akte Nora S.," work is a necessity of life,
"das erste Lebensbedürfnis" for the heroine Nora. In order to be able to
complete her task, she sacrifices her love relationship with Färber, and later
with Likendeel. Moreover, she does not shirk hardships, but stays at the
geological site high up on the mountain, until she has found the cause of the

---

[24]   Karl Marx and Friedrich Engels, *Werke* (Berlin: Dietz, 1962), XIX, 21.
[25]   "Der positive Held im sozialistischen Realismus und der neue Charakter der Arbeit,"
p. 937.

malfunctioning of the pumps she designed. She sets a high standard for herself in her work. When she is misunderstood because she does not give in to the short-sighted demands of the firm employing her, she still does not give up her self-appointed task of designing better pumps, in spite of the opposition she meets.

Nora, like Kast, is presented as a progressive individual, seemingly ahead of her time. Her devotion to her work is outstanding and exemplary. In another variation and interpretation of Karl Marx's statement, Heinz Plavius observes that one of the characteristics of socialism and communism is "die Arbeit zum ersten Lebensbedürfnis zu machen, weil nur auf dieser Grundlage allseitig entwickelte Persönlichkeiten entstehen können."[26] Volker Braun's hero Kast, Erik Neutsch's heroine Nora, and Werner Bräunig's heroes Hannes Stütz and Peter Trumm are examples of individuals in whose lives work has a central place; they have, at the same time, well-developed socialist personalities.

[26] Ibid., p. 943.

Chapter II

THE COLLECTIVE

Closely connected with the significance of work in the new society is the collective, which, according to the *Kultur-politisches Wörterbuch*,[1] is "Ausdruck und Form der entwickelten sozialistischen Arbeitsweise und sozialistischer Beziehungen des menschlichen Zusammenlebens" (pp. 269–70). The various relationships of the individual to his work and to the other members of his society are usually linked in some way to a collective; it is part of the very fabric of socialist society:

> Im entwickelten sozialistischen Gesellschaftssystem wird das K. zur herrschenden Form gesellschaftlicher Tätigkeit – in der Arbeit, im demokratischen Leben, im Studium, in der Weiterbildung, in Forschungsgemeinschaften sowie in den Einheiten der bewaffneten Organe. (ibid., p. 270)

Thus most of the social and political activities of the individual are part of a collective.

In the GDR, work is invariably seen as taking place within a social setting, because of the socialist concept that the cause of alienation has been removed from the life of the worker by the socialist revolution, and that the workers are now equal. The collective is the specific organizational form of such a community of workers in a socialist society; it expresses their unity and their interaction as they gather around a common purpose and activity.

It has an organic unity; "Kollektive sind nicht ein Haufen von Leuten, sondern Gruppen von Menschen, die sich um eine Aufgabe scharen und diese Aufgabe mit höchstem Effekt zum Ziele führen,"[2] observes Evamaria Nahke. The unity of the group is always centred around a common task. "Ist die Aufgabe erfüllt," she points out, "entsteht sofort das Bedürfnis einer anderen Gruppierung, stehen andere konkrete Bewährungsgegenstände an und mit ihnen ein neues Zusammenfinden und neue konkrete Menschenentwicklungen" (ibid. p. 732).

Besides facilitating the completion of a common task, the collective constitutes a vital social unit in which the individual is able to find himself and to develop his full potential. In his essay "Unsere neue Wirklichkeit literarisch erobern,"[3] Arno Hochmuth observes: "Die Entfaltung des Individuums mit all seinen Talenten, Fähigkeiten und Möglichkeiten erfolgt nicht im Alleingang,

---

[1]   Berlin: Dietz, 1970.
[2]   "Arbeit an den großen Gegenständen unserer Zeit. Gespräch mit Benito Wogatzki," *WB*, 15, No. 4 (1969), 732.
[3]   In *Kritik in der Zeit*.

sondern immer im Rahmen bestimmter Kollektive und Gemeinschaften" (p. 815). Even personal relationships like friendships and family ties are strongly influenced by the collective. In the new society, it constitutes the setting for the individual's interactions with others and his relationships.

In many *Erzählungen* and *Kurzgeschichten,* the collective, its significance and its role in the life of the individual, are depicted. Writers of the GDR regard it as their task to describe collectives, and in doing so, to develop models, which the working population, which is called upon to form such a collective, can understand and visualize. Arno Hochmuth, in the essay mentioned above, comments on the portrayal of the collective in the literature of the GDR:

> Den Einfluß des Kollektivs auf das Mitglied, die Rückwirkung des einzelnen auf das Kollektiv ästhetisch zu erfassen und nacherlebbar zu machen, ist gewiß eine der kompliziertesten, aber auch dankbarsten Aufgaben für den Gegenwartsschriftsteller. (ibid.)

Werner Bräunig also mentions the significance of this theme: "Die Kollektivität unserer Gesellschaft: sie ist ins Zentrum der Darstellung gerückt."[4]

The model collective

Two *Erzählungen* by Werner Bräunig portray model collectives; they present the every-day world of the worker, but from an ideal point of view, and the problems that arise are solved in an exemplary way. In Bräunig's "Gewöhnliche Leute," the hero Hannes Stütz, a construction engineer, works together with his collective to complete a difficult task. He marshalls all the resources available to him and secures the co-operation of every person concerned. He turns to other workers who are more experienced, or are specialists in the field, for advice and help: "Er hatte sich nach bewährtem Muster an alle gewandt, die die Sache anging. Sie kannten die kritischen Wege und konnten voraussagen, was geschehen mußte, wenn etwas erreicht wurde oder nicht erreicht" (p. 52). He also co-operates with Sandmann, the construction engineer from a neighbouring site, because he has realized: "Es ging nicht gut ohneeinander, gegeneinander ging es manchmal besser, am besten jedoch ging es miteinander" (p. 53). At the end, Stütz is successful in his experiment to finish the building a hundred and twenty days ahead of schedule. This feat became possible because the members of the collective worked well together and shared their knowledge and experience.

---

[4] *Prosa schreiben: Anmerkungen zum Realismus* (Halle/Saale: Mitteldeutscher Verlag, 1968), p. 24.

Similarly, the *Erzählung* "Der schöne Monat August" by Bräunig shows how the members of a collective can work together, thus increasing and multiplying the resources of the individual, and it shows how each person's involvement in accomplishing a common task creates a powerful unity and organic wholeness in the group. The hero Peter Trumm, or "Trumpeter," a caterpillar operator, takes the initiative in an emergency situation by making a daring suggestion to his fellow workers, which saves their excavation from being hopelessly flooded. His plan is successful because of the co-operation of all concerned:

> Trumpeter hatte sich allerhand ausgerechnet, aber eine solche Wirkung hätte auch er nicht für möglich gehalten. Der ganze Tiefbau war von einem wilden Arbeitsfieber erfaßt, niemand wartete auf Anweisungen, alle taten genau das Richtige im richtigen Moment und in einem Tempo, das noch keiner erlebt hatte. (pp. 135–36)

A spirit of enthusiasm and excitement imbues the collective, enabling each individual to do his utmost. In harmony with his fellow workers, each man knows instinctively what to do and is able to do it quickly and effectively. In this *Erzählung,* Bräunig depicts the co-operation of the workers in the collective as an emotional experience, not just as an intellectual concept.

A model collective is also portrayed in Jurij Brězan's story "Kein romantisches Verhältnis."[5] Here, too, the impossible is achieved as the workers co-operate in the building of a suitable gymnasium for the "Arbeiterfestspiele," which has to be completed within a short period of time. They succeed splendidly; the whole corporate effort of building is presented as a kind of game, which is won because everyone does his share. All of these *Erzählungen* are optimistic, and though they are firmly based on a realistic description of the worker's world, they suggest how the collective should function in the new society.

Another type of narrative portrays how an individual is convinced and made aware of the necessity and desirability of joining a collective. A decisive change in the protagonist's attitude is brought about by some event, which, at the same time, is the climax of the story. In the *Erzählung* "Felix verliert eine Wette"[6] by Joachim Nowotny, the heroine, a young city-bred girl, "das Kindergartenmädchen," finds difficulty in adjusting to her unaccustomed surroundings and village life. She feels isolated and finally decides to leave. But in an emergency situation, she realizes how badly her services are needed to look after the children, so that the mothers will be freed to help save the potato crop. The pride that had kept her isolated melts, and she whole-

---

[5] In *Der Mäuseturm* (Berlin: Verlag Neues Leben, 1970).
[6] In *Labyrinth ohne Schrecken: Erzählungen* (Halle/Saale: Mitteldeutscher Verlag, 1967).

heartedly chooses to help the people of the village and to become one of them by joining their collective.

The story "Das Rindenschiff,"[7] also by Joachim Nowotny, resembles a parable; hence, it represents another way of portraying the theme of the model collective. Like the other *Erzählungen,* it emphasizes the importance of individuals working together in achieving a common goal, but the concept is presented symbolically. A small boat carved by a little boy is helped along in its course by various persons, by Jonas, who is cleaning up the ditch, by Oma Slabke coming to dip for water, by Professor Funkenburg, who is fishing. The boat becomes the symbol of the unity of those who co-operate to make its progress possible: "Es wird schon ans Ziel kommen, denken wir, bestimmt kommt es an. Hauptsache, es finden sich immer wieder Menschen, die ihm weiter helfen. Wirst du dabeisein? " (p. 279). The aim of the story is to cultivate an awareness of the essential importance of each individual's contribution to the larger whole, the collective.

In the *Erzählungen* about the model collective, the following points are generally emphasized: that a task is achieved more quickly and efficiently by a collective; however, this depends on the whole-hearted involvement of each individual. In Erik Neutsch's *Erzählung* "Drei Tage unseres Lebens," the Party secretary Werner Konz declares: "Natürlich schaffen wir's nur, wenn alle an einem Strang ziehen . . . Allein ist der Tod" (p. 134). Another point is that the strength and effectiveness of the individual worker to accomplish a particular task is multiplied, when he is part of a collective.

Finally, a third point is that the individual has to learn to submit to, and to participate in, the necessary give-and-take that is required in a collective. In the *Erzählung* by Erik Neutsch, "Drei Tage unseres Lebens," Party secretary Konz is willing to give up his own plan and to consider an alternative one offered by the chief architect Koblenz. They are able to compromise, and, in this way, to arrive at the best solution of all. "Wer in der hochorganisierten und vielfältig verflochtenen Welt der sozialistischen Systembeziehungen schöpferisch wirken will," observes Elisabeth Simons, "kann das nur in größerem Rahmen, in kollektivem Handeln mit anderen und damit durch Einordnen tun."[8]

Taking the step "vom Ich zum Wir"

In the *Erzählungen* and *Kurzgeschichten* of the GDR, the individual is generally presented as one who overcomes his own interests and becomes part of a community of workers. The main emphasis is always on the increasing

---

[7]   In *Labyrinth ohne Schrecken.*
[8]   " 'Das Andersmachen, von Grund auf,' " p. 193.

importance of the collective in the life of the individual. Many stories deal with a change of attitude which the individual undergoes in the new society: from a feeling of being a single individual, an "I," as it were, he emerges with a sense of belonging to a group, of being part of a "we." Elisabeth Simons speaks of the "Ichbezogenheit" of the individual, which is overcome as his socialist personality develops within the process of interacting with the other members of the collective: "Die menschliche Persönlichkeit entfaltet sich nur in lebendiger Anteilnahme an ihrer gesellschaftlichen Umgebung und im Überwinden der engen Ichbezogenheit."[9] This process of consciously becoming a member of a collective through active participation in it is portrayed in various ways in a number of *Erzählungen.*

As the socialist consciousness of Adele Noth, the heroine of Werner Bräunig's "Gewöhnliche Leute," grows and develops in her active life and relationships in the new society, her sense of solidarity and oneness with her collective grows, too. Her childhood had been difficult, for her father, a Nazi, had been removed after the war from his post as the manager of a factory, and thus her family were outsiders socially and ideologically. However, as Adele grew up in a socialist society and went to school and to university, and as she took up her work at the construction site, she overcame her isolation and became one with the collective: "Sie gehörte nun dazu" (p. 19). Her love-affair with Hannes Stütz only serves to consolidate this fact. Her relationships with her fellow workers at the construction site, as, for example, her friends the Moßmanns, constitute her new family ties. The author says of Adele:

> Manchmal, vor vielen Jahren war sie allein gewesen. Später waren die anderen da, zu denen sie gehörte, mit denen sie in den Hörsälen dieses Landes saß, die Bücher dieses Landes las, mit denen sie sich stritt und manchmal böse war, mit denen sie lernte. Es war nicht immer leicht gewesen . . . Aber es war gut. . . . Und allein gewesen war sie von da an nicht mehr. (p. 45)

As she starts to participate in the life of a collective, first of the one at her university and then of the one at the construction site, a new and rich life begins for her. Instead of standing alone, she can now contribute her talents and training fully to the building up of the socialist society of which she has consciously become a part.

In her essay " 'Das Andersmachen, von Grund auf,' " Elisabeth Simons speaks of "das gesellschaftliche Ich,"[10] which characterizes the new man who is wholly aware of the collective, who has taken the "Schritt vom Ich zum Wir" (ibid., pp. 192–93). The readiness of the individual for the collective depends on his maturity, which is consonant with a well-developed socialist personality.

---

[9]   Ibid., p. 191.
[10] Ibid., p. 188.

Tolja, the hero of Werner Heiduczek's *Erzählung Mark Aurel oder ein Semester Zärtlichkeit*,[11] is not yet mature enough to break through his self-centredness. He is caught up in a state of vacillation, in which, on the one hand, he is aware of his predicament and wishes to break through his isolation, speaking, as he does, "von dem 'verdammten Ich,' aus dem man doch herauskommen muß" (p. 63), and, on the other hand, he insists on his individuality and prides himself on his originality. "Tolja wollte mir immer weismachen, man könne auch allein aus sich heraus leben" (p. 96), observes Yana. His self-preoccupation and his lack of a socialist consciousness lead to his ruin, for he is finally expelled from university and his relationship with Yana breaks down irreparably. She finally has to tell him: "Leb, wie du willst, ich kann so nicht leben" (p. 137). His personality deteriorates, for, as Elisabeth Simons observes, the development of personality is only possible in the collective and in doing one's work in it.[12]

Tolja is not able to assume a responsible place in the collective; when he is given a job in a factory, at which he is to prove himself for a year, he leaves after three weeks. Moreover, he is self-centred and immature, and wishes others to think of him as being extraordinary: "Er konnte nicht mehr leben, ohne als außergewöhnlich zu gelten" (p. 126). Caught up in his isolation, he is unable to consider the needs and wishes of others. "Alle sollen für dich dasein," Yana tells him. "Du kümmerst dich um niemanden" (p. 131). There is no room for such an individual in a socialist society, because he does not fit into a collective.

The readiness of a person to participate in the life of a collective depends on the degree to which his socialist personality has developed. This, in turn, depends on the individual's commitment to his work and his collective. In the literature of the GDR most of the characters are depicted as being determined by this commitment, which usually forms the basis of their relationship to the new society. The stories frequently express the unity of the collective and the individual. "Die Hauptgestalten sind in komplizierten und festen sozialen Beziehungen erfaßt. Ihrem intellektuellen und ethischen Reifegrad entspricht das Gefühl der Verbundenheit des individuellen Schicksals mit dem Schicksal aller,"[13] observes Elisabeth Simons. This is true of Adele Noth, as it is of Yana, the heroine of Werner Heiduczek's *Erzählung*, even though for a while she is almost carried off course by Tolja's influence and his capacity to fascinate her.

At an early age, Yana was made aware of her self-centredness and expressed a desire to overcome it. Her teacher told her: "Dein Egozentrismus wird dir noch mal das Genick brechen. Du mußt dir Mühe geben, auch an die anderen zu denken. Du lebst ja nicht allein auf der Welt" (pp. 37–38). Yana made every

---

[11]   Berlin: Verlag Neues Leben, 1971.
[12]   " 'Das Andersmachen, von Grund auf,' " p. 191.
[13]   Ibid., p. 186.

effort to better herself: "Ich setzte Tage fest, an denen ich nur an die anderen denken wollte. Ich übernahm Patenschaften, leitete den Russisch-Zirkel und wurde Rettungsschwimmer. . . . Ich hatte das Verlangen, mich den anderen ganz hinzugeben" (p. 38). However, she realizes that her youthful efforts were, as she says, "nur eine andere Form meiner Ichsucht. . . . Ich tat alles aus der Gier nach Anerkennung, nicht aus dem Begreifen einer Verantwortung" (p. 39). Nevertheless, she grows up to be a well-integrated member of her collective and the new society. She recovers from her nervous breakdown, a result of her unhappy love affair with Tolja, when she decides to rejoin her collective. She even cancels the holiday at a resort prescribed for her by her doctor to be able to return to the university sooner. She thus affirms the priority of the collective in her life.

The lesson which she learns is also mentioned by Kast in Volker Braun's *Erzählung Das ungezwungne Leben Kasts:* "Es geht keinem von uns nur um sich, dachte ich, es geht um die Entwicklung der Verhältnisse, die mehr braucht als was einer mit sich macht, die nur in gemeinsamer Arbeit geschieht, die wir suchen!" (p. 128). His own development is an ever deeper involvement in the collective, and in the overcoming of his isolation, which he felt acutely at the beginning of the story. Through his experience of working side by side with the other members of his brigade, he is enabled to take the step "vom Ich zum Wir."

In most *Erzählungen,* the individual who has to overcome his self-centredness is a young person. An exception is the old man in Werner Bräunig's *Erzählung* "Stillegung." He fears the threat of becoming isolated in his retirement, and therefore he takes up new employment as a night watchman to feel again that he is part of a collective. Thus, in many ways, the observation made in Pracht and Neubert can be corroborated: "Äußerst vielfältig waren die Anlässe, Begebenheiten und persönliche Erlebnisse, durch die der einzelne die Impulse empfing, den Weg vom Ich zum Wir einzuschlagen" (p. 127).

The characters, who have undergone the development from the self-centred individual to become members of a collective, express a feeling of belonging and unity with others, which had hitherto been unknown to them. In Volker Braun's *Das ungezwungne Leben Kasts,* the hero feels differently after he has overcome his "Ichbezogenheit": "Ich steckte in einer anderen Haut. Ich empfand alles um mich deutlicher und für mich wichtig" (p. 47). Overcoming his selfish interests, he can now look beyond himself and is brought closer to others. "Dieses neue Gefühl drängte mich, alles zu umfassen . . ." (ibid.), he exclaims. At another point in the narrative, he cries: "Ja, ich fühlte die Freude, mit vielen Freund zu sein, diese Freude würde ich nie verlieren aus der Brust" (p. 100).

In Werner Bräunig's "Der schöne Monat August," the protagonist Peter Trumm works feverishly with the rest of his collective to accomplish a heroic deed; he observes: "An solchen Tagen weiß man plötzlich, ob man sich in einer

Mannschaft befindet oder bloß in einem Haufen einzelner" (p. 131). A group-feeling, an identification on the part of each individual with the collective, emerges as they work together. At the same time, each person gains a heightened sense of self. "Schon eher geht es darum, daß einer nur ganz bei sich selber sein kann, wenn er zugleich ganz bei seinen Leuten ist" (p. 125), remarks Peter Trumm. Thus, a particular feeling or consciousness, which the individual has as a member of a collective, is suggested in these *Erzählungen*.

The motif of responsibility

Closely associated with the individual's commitment to the collective is his responsibility to it. This motif runs through a number of *Erzählungen*. In his essay "Persönlichkeit und Gemeinschaft in der sozialistischen Gesellschaft," Günter Heyden observes that among the essential qualities of character revealed by a member of the new society is "vor allem hohes Pflicht- und Verantwortungsbewußtsein."[14]

In his *Erzählung Mark Aurel oder ein Semester Zärtlichkeit,* Werner Heiduczek uses the term "social responsibility." When Yana has to decide whether she should study in Leningrad, which would mean leaving her boy-friend Walter, or stay at home, she is is told: "Über eines sollten Sie sich im klaren sein, eine solche Entscheidung ist nicht allein etwas Privates. Es gibt so etwas wie gesellschaftliche Verantwortung, für einen jungen Menschen genauso wie für einen älteren" (pp. 55–56). Even in such an apparently personal decision, the individual has to consider his responsibility to the collective.

In the same *Erzählung,* the hero Tolja possesses no sense of "gesellschaftliche Verantwortung". Instead of considering his duty to the collective, he blames others for his shortcomings. "Du machst es dir sehr einfach," says Yana. "Schuld sind immer die anderen. Alle sollen für dich dasein. Du kümmerst dich um niemanden" (p. 131). His sense of being part of the collective, and, consequently, his socialist consciousness and feeling of responsibility are deficient. Selfishly, he thinks only of what suits him and thus leaves the job that was given to him after he was expelled from the university, simply because he finds it too dull. Yana is upset about his action: "Wenn du nach drei Wochen schon aus dem Kombinat fortläufst, lassen sie dich überhaupt nicht mehr studieren ... Wie soll man dir glauben, daß du etwas durchhältst" (p. 121). She talks to him about "Verantwortung im Leben" (ibid.), and that he has to change. Tolja is an example of an individual who lacks a proper sense of responsibility to his collective and is thus at odds with the life of the new society.

[14]   *Deutsche Zeitschrift für Philosophie,* p. 11.

The word responsibility occurs frequently in Benito Wogatzki's *Erzählung* "Ein Tag und eine Nacht." The hero of this *Erzählung* is a model of the responsible individual in the new society. The other characters, for example Ursula and Willi, whose socialist consciousness is not as well developed, stand out in contrast. As the boss of the work brigade, or "brigadier," the hero feels responsible not only for the "Zyklogramm," which is their plan for the co-ordination of all activities on the construction site, but also for the people and their relationships with each other, because he knows that the inter-personal relationships of the workers have to be good, if the work is to go well. Thus he is not only the boss, but also a teacher and friend. Moreover, his own private life and his duties at work are closely intertwined. He does not hesitate to sacrifice his own comfort and well-deserved rest in order to help others. The collective is most important to him, and thus private and public interests merge for him. When Wandeck, his superior, asks him to come even a little earlier to start his shift, the brigadier, who has lost most of his sleep taking care of Ursula and her child, replies: "Ja . . . ich werde etwas früher kommen. Es liegt ja in meinem ureigensten Interesse" (p. 401).

Willi, one of the other workers in the brigade, lacks the proper sense of responsibility. He does not bother to find out who the girl was whom he took home from the dance: "Ich hab mich doch nie gefragt, wann oder woher so ein Mädel kommt. Was geht mich das auch an? ! Sie mußte doch wissen . . ." (p. 414). "Und nun saß er drin in diesem Verantwortungsdreck" (ibid.), comments the narrator. The brigadier tries to teach him a lesson and to make him aware of the implications of his action. Willi refuses to listen: "Mich geht das alles nichts an. Du bist hier falsch! Ich bin weder für den Jungen zuständig noch für dieses Dingsda, dieses Zyklogramm!" (p. 415). However, through the efforts of the brigadier, he finally gains sufficient insight to change his course of action.

Selflessly, the brigadier goes without sleep, takes care of the little boy for whom nobody else has time, and tries to talk to Ursula. He is even willing to be slandered and to be misunderstood, taking the blame upon himself, so that the marriage of Ham and Ursula will be saved. At last, the "Zyklogramm," endangered by human weakness, can function without disruption. "Man muß das Ganze sehen" (p. 417), he remarks. "Das Ganze" is the common purpose ("das Zyklogramm") and the private life and actions of those who work at it, two things which for him are impossible to separate. He comments wryly: "Ich will. . . daß man sich eine ganz entfernte Vorstellung davon machen soll, wie einem Verantwortlichen zumute ist, der bestimmte Beschlüsse kennt . . . und eine wahnsinnige Nachtschicht hinter sich hat . . ." (p. 368). He represents the man who is truly responsible for his collective.

The collective as mentor

A collective, as, for example, a brigade of workers or a student body, may act as mentor or advisor to one of its members. Yana, the heroine of Werner Heiduczek's *Erzählung Mark Aurel oder ein Semester Zärtlichkeit*, takes someone else's chemical instrument, because there is always a long line-up for supplies and she needs it immediately. "Am nächsten Tag gab es meinetwegen eine Gruppenversammlung. Ich sollte sagen, was mit mir los sei" (p. 105), declares Yana. As a result, her situation is clarified and she is helped.

The collective helps to correct the individual who may be acting in ways contrary to accepted moral standards of the new society. It criticizes him, advises him, and helps him to solve his personal problems. One of the ten moral principles of socialism, first proclaimed by Walter Ulbricht at the "V. Parteitag" of the SED in 1958, reads: "Du sollst beim Aufbau des Sozialismus im Geiste der gegenseitigen Hilfe und der kameradschaftlichen Zusammenarbeit handeln, das Kollektiv achten und seine Kritik beherzigen."[15] Thus, the worker is reminded to get along with and help his fellow workers and to listen to the advice and criticism of the group.

In Jurij Brězan's narrative "Kein romantisches Verhältnis," the electrical workers, who have done an inferior job in wiring the new sports arena, are reminded by the other workers of the high quality of the carpenters' work, with the result that they decide to redo their work:

> Also jene Bautzener Elektriker betrachten das Tischlerwerk, stumm oder nicht stumm, das weiß man nicht, aber weil gleich danach Frühstückspause war, gingen sie in sich, verhältnismäßig laut, habe ich mir erzählen lassen, und dann rissen sie ihre Leitungen wieder aus der Wand, und am Abend konnte jeder sehen, daß schlechte Beispiele durch gute Sitten aus der Welt geschafft werden können. (p. 94)

The incident is told in a humorous way, but the moral is unmistakeable; in this *Erzählung* those who do inferior work are reminded that they do so at the expense of others, and in realizing this, they feel the necessity to improve.

The question, however, is also brought up as to what extent the collective is responsible for helping and guiding the individual in his private affairs. This question occupies Peter Trumm's mind in Werner Bräunig's *Erzählung* "Der schöne Monat August," in connection with Lehnert, one of the workers in his brigade, who has personal problems. Trumm, as the boss of the brigade, has tried to speak to him and to advise him about his marital problems, but finds it difficult. He knows that he himself can cope with all kinds of difficulties connected with his work. "Aber wer ist schon auf so was eingerichtet? " he

[15]   Bernd Bittighöfer and Jürgen Schmollack, eds., *Moral und Gesellschaft: Entwicklungsprobleme der sozialistischen Moral in der DDR* (Berlin: Dietz, 1968), p. 30.

thinks. "Um die Kinder wird sich die Schule kümmern, um den Mann die Brigade — aber was denn nun noch alles? " (p. 102). He decides: " 'Man darf den Spaß auch nicht übertreiben.' Irgend etwas muß schließlich bleiben, was die Leute gefälligst mit sich selber abmachen. Das war sein letztes Wort" (ibid.). Thus, the author implies that a certain margin should be left for privacy in an individual's life.

Loyalty to the collective and the claims of family life

In Volker Braun's *Erzählung Das ungezwungne Leben Kasts,* the protagonist observes,

> es komme alles auf die Gemeinschaft an, nur in ihr entwickle sich wer, das sei ein und dasselbe — in der Gruppe begännen eben die Bindungen, die dann hinaustreiben, dafür müßten wir alles aus uns herausholen und uns nicht beschränken in die eigne Haut . . . (p. 65)

This is one of the basic ideas that the stories reveal. The individual needs the collective, which gives him a sense of identity, of belonging to a group, and which furthers his development of a socialist consciousness.

As the individual identifies more and more with the interests of the group, family ties and personal relationships begin to recede into the background, or take on a different significance for the person concerned. The question arises: does loyalty to the collective take precedence over family ties?

Three different solutions to problems connected with love relationships are found in three *Erzählungen;* however, in all of them the collective plays a significant role. In the relationship of Hannes Stütz and Adele Noth in "Gewöhnliche Leute" by Werner Bräunig, the collective acts as a catalyst in which their love blossoms and is strengthened. Adele Noth is a newcomer to the construction site; however, it does not take long before she feels that she belongs to it. This sense of belonging is reinforced by her love for Hannes: "Nun war sie auf eine neue Art nicht allein, nicht zu trennen von jener, aber doch anders" (p. 45). There is complete harmony between her relationship to Stütz, constituting a new family tie, as it were, and the collective. Hannes Stütz, too, feels that his love for Adele is right, and he is at peace with himself:

> Und dann dachte er: Diesmal ist es richtig. Er hätte das keinem erklären können, aber er war ganz und gar sicher. Diesmal ist es das Richtige. Auch er war diesmal der Richtige. Er hatte eine Tür gefunden. Denn auch das gehört dazu. Daß einer weiß, wer er ist. Daß er weiß, wer er sein kann. Daß er unterwegs bleibt zu sich und den anderen. (p. 32)

Their love helps to reinforce their good relationship with the collective, and vice versa, the collective supports and consolidates their relationship to each other.

In Werner Heiduczek's *Erzählung Mark Aurel oder ein Semester Zärtlichkeit,* on the other hand, the love relationship between Yana and Tolja acts as a disrupting force, and Yana has to give it up in order to make her former good relationship with the collective possible again; her devotion to Tolja had made her blind to the interests of the collective. "Die anderen sind für dich ein Dreck, wenn nur deinem Tolja nichts passiert," she is told. "Alles, was du siehst, siehst du nur noch durch ihn. Wer gegen Tolja ist, ist schlecht. Wer etwas gegen ihn sagt, hat unrecht" (p. 112). Yana admits: "Mein Empfinden für Tolja drängte alles zurück. Ich war sehr eng geworden" (p. 113). She has to separate herself from Tolja before she can once again become a part of the collective, because Tolja, who has a poorly developed socialist consciousness, acts as a hindrance.

In Volker Braun's *Erzählung Das ungezwungne Leben Kasts,* the protagonist sees marriage to Linde as an impediment to his freedom to develop his ties to the collective. The author uses the word "binden" for both relationships. Kast tells Linde, "daß . . . [er sich] nicht an sie binden könne" (p. 101). Moreover, he speaks of her "Bindungssucht" (p. 94), and he complains: "Ihre Hingabe, die mich fast ängstigte, band mich mit aller Gewalt an sie . . ." (p. 71). On the other hand, he is challenged by the tasks he has to do together with others, which bind him to the collective: "Das war viel verlangt; aber es machte uns Spaß, viel von uns zu verlangen — und für Aufgaben zu leben, die uns immer mehr und mit *vielen* verbinden würden!" (p. 65). He also speaks of "die Vielfalt dieser Bindungen" (p. 64) in connection with his work and his collective. He wants to be committed to many people and to the collective, but he shies away from the commitment to Linde, who wants him to marry her.

These *Erzählungen* suggest that the collective forms the basis of a personal relationship. When the support of the collective is lacking, when one of the individuals does not have a well-developed socialist consciousness or is selfish, interested only in having a private affair, the relationship does not have a sufficient basis. Then the more progressive individual has to choose in favour of the collective, as Yana in Heiduczek's *Erzählung* and Braun's hero Kast have done.

Manfred Jendryschik, in his *Kurzgeschichte* "Fahren,"[16] portrays an individual who puts the interests of the collective above his immediate private concerns. Only a few hours after the funeral of his twenty-three-year-old daughter, the protagonist Kramer has to keep a commitment and go off on a business trip. He does not question the precedence of duty over his private

---

[16] In *Glas und Ahorn.*

feelings, but does what is expected of him. The Party secretary expects him to go as a matter of course, and Redloff, Kramer's superior, reminds him of his duty:

> Natürlich hatte Krack, der Parteisekretär, gesagt, er müsse fahren, gar keine Diskussion, und Redloff hatte getobt, seit wann Privatsachen, schließlich hätte er Kramer, den Kran zu steuern, zu erklären, und dann waren Worte gefallen von Vertragstreue und Warschauer Pakt. (p. 160)

Only one member of the collective objects:

> Erich Holtenstieg hatte ihm widersprochen, diesmal, mit wenigen Sätzen, und Redloff hatte den Raum verlassen, sich später aber entschuldigt. Alle hatten im Kursbuch geblättert, die günstigste Verbindung herausgeknobelt, dann war er in einem Werkswagen zur Stadt gefahren worden. (ibid.)

The rest of the collective show their sympathy and concern for him, as well as their support of his carrying out his duty, by helping him to get ready for his trip and taking him to the station. Thus, the demands and interests of the larger whole, of the state and the collective, are given first priority.

In his discussion of the *Kurzgeschichte* "Fahren," Heinz Plavius observes:

> Nun gab es Stimmen im Betrieb, nicht zu fahren – und während der Rückfahrt reflektiert er über diese Diskussion, gleichsam andeutend, wie selbstverständlich in unserer Gesellschaft ein solcher Konflikt zwischen gesellschaftlichen und individuellen Interessen zu einer Lösung geführt werden kann.[17]

This statement is in accordance with the socialist ideal, which is, as Elisabeth Simons emphasizes in her essay " 'Das Andersmachen, von Grund auf,' " the "Übereinstimmung der gesellschaftlichen und individuellen Interessen . . ." (p. 198), and "die Bereitschaft des einzelnen zu freiwilliger Disziplin und aktiver Selbsterziehung . . ." (ibid.). As indicated by Elisabeth Simons, the ideal of the new society is the submerging of one's own interests in those of the collective. She says: "Nicht der Anspruch auf Glück, sondern das Vermögen, in produktiver Hinwendung zur Gemeinschaft echtes Glück zu finden, macht die sozialistische Persönlichkeit aus" (ibid., p. 200).

Two *Erzählungen,* Erik Neutsch's "Drei Tage unseres Lebens," and Benito Wogatzki's "Ein Tag und eine Nacht," show the ideal unity of private life and the life of the collective. There is an identity of interests that is evident in the character and life of the heroes and their actions, which are wholly orientated towards the collective. In "Drei Tage unseres Lebens," the Party secretary Werner Konz's social and private interests appear to be the same; he is single-mindedly engaged in working out the problems of his group. Only at the

---

[17] "Gestalt und Gestaltung . . . ," p. 153.

end of the story does Brüdering discover anything about his private life. Similarly, Benito Wogatzki's brigadier in "Ein Tag und eine Nacht" makes the interests of the collective his own. He is deeply concerned over the welfare of each member of his brigade, helping Ham with his personal problems and trying to show Willi, who lacks a socialist consciousness, his duty to others. They are, as it were, his family, and thus, his private interests and the interests of the collective merge for him.

The individual as a private person

Some writers of short prose narratives have shown an awareness of the individual in the new society as a private person, portraying his inner world and aspects of life that are outside of the collective. *Erzählungen* and *Kurzgeschichten* of this kind, too, are within the tradition of the literature of the GDR, though they occupy a much less significant place.

In the *Erzählungen* of the GDR, the literary character is usually presented as being part of a group of some kind; however, in Günter Kunert's *Kurzgeschichte* "Fahrt mit der S-Bahn,"[18] the individual is alone; even when he rides in a crowded "S-Bahn," he is not part of a crowd. He eagerly watches for a lighted window that he saw in a drab wall on an earlier trip along the same route. He longs for his friends, whom he perceived for a fleeting moment in that lighted room conversing with him. These are not necessarily those who came close to him as they worked side by side at a common task, but simply friends who had shared a part of his life and were dear to him. They belong to his world as individuals in their own right, not necessarily as members of a collective in the new society. "Fahrt mit der S-Bahn" is told more as a flight of the imagination, than in a realistic vein, for, although the "S-Bahn" itself is re-created faithfully, the lighted window is a creation of the imagination, an expression of his longing. "Könnte ich ein einziges Mal dort eintreten und mich vereinigen mit mir . . . so wäre alles ungeschehen, was die Wagenladungen von Worten niemals zudecken werden," muses the protagonist. "Einmal im richtigen Moment eintreten, und ich wäre erlöst" (p. 68). These words, somewhat ambiguous, but certainly expressing a longing for a personal identity, suggest other needs of the person than those usually found in the *Erzählungen* of socialist realism.

Similarly, Christa Wolf's story "Juninachmittag,"[19] presents facets and values of private life which are not necessarily identical with those of the

[18] In *Kramen in Fächern: Geschichten, Parabeln, Merkmale,* 2nd ed. (Berlin: Aufbau-Verlag, 1972).
[19] In *Fahrt mit der S-Bahn: Erzähler der DDR,* ed. Lutz-W. Wolff (München: dtv 778, 1971).

collective. The author re-creates a leisurely afternoon in a garden spent together by a family. The outside world, suggested by the planes crossing overhead, by the visits of the neighbours, by the school experiences of one of the daughters, and by the references to the railroad accident and other news told by the neighbours, is very much present; however, the focal point is the personal interaction of the members of the family. The family and the circle of neighbours are, perhaps, a kind of collective; however, their bond is based on pleasure in each others's company, or the casual interactions that draw them together, rather than on being engaged in working side by side in a factory or a construction site for some material goal, as the majority of the other stories show.

In the *Erzählung* "Juninachmittag," a person is important for his own sake, regardless of his function in society. The author suggests the fragility and vulnerability, as well as the strength, of the individual. The reference to the railroad accident develops the idea of the vulnerability of man. One of the victims is the actor's wife who often passed by the garden with her dogs: "Jene Frau, von der man nur noch die Handtasche gefunden hatte, sah und hörte auch nichts mehr. In welchem Spiel sie ihre Hände auch gehabt haben mochte, man hatte sie ihr weggeschlagen, und das Spiel ging ohne sie weiter" (p. 245). The transience of life is evoked by this statement, which is referred to again at the conclusion of the *Erzählung:* "Wer sagt denn, daß der Arm schon unaufhaltsam ausgeholt hat zu dem Schlag, der einem die Hände aus allem herausreißt? Wer sagt denn, daß diesmal wir gemeint sind? Daß das Spiel ohne uns weiterginge? " (p. 246). It is further evoked by the reference to the rose, "die nur heute und morgen noch außen gelb und innen rosa ist" (ibid.), and to the passing day: "Der sinkende Tag, sagt man ja. Warum soll man nicht spüren können, wie er sinkt: vorbei an der Sonne . . ." (p. 245).

The *Erzählung* suggests situations in life which a person has to face alone. Human values which affect, and which shape, a person's life, coupled with his own attitude and decisions, which are not just pragmatic and considered to be for the good of the community, are presented. The kindliness and generosity of a Frau B. are shown, and a child's sense of wonder, as well as the tensions and excitement of the adolescent at the threshold of adulthood, are captured in this *Erzählung* by Christa Wolf.

In his *Erzählung Mark Aurel oder ein Semester Zärtlichkeit,* Werner Heiduczek deals to a large extent with the inner life and the personal problems of the individual and his relationship to others, showing the difficulties he may encounter, which may be too complex for him to cope with himself or for others to help. Yana observes: "Die Geschichte mit Tolja hat mich ganz schön geschmissen. Ich glaube, das Studienjahr ist futsch" (p. 10). Her family, though considerate and loving, can only stand on the side and wait: "Meine Schwester erzählt mir jeden Tag, wie leise sie jetzt am Morgen sind, seit das mit mir passiert ist und ich zu Hause bin" (p. 7). Yana, who calls herself "langweilig normal" (p. 24), has always been a well-adjusted member of the new society, but in trying to cope with her disappointment in love, another side of her, the strictly personal and private one, comes to the fore, and she has to learn to deal with it and to make her own decisions in regard to it.

Werner Heiduczek speaks of the "Widersprüchlichkeit im Menschen,"[20] especially in a young person; he remarks: "Jeder weiß um dieses Widersprüchliche in sich und um sich" (ibid.). He suggests that the answers pertaining to the individual and his relationship to himself and others are not always obvious and easy to find. In his *Erzählung Mark Aurel oder ein Semester Zärtlichkeit,* Yana says of her literature teacher:

> Ich glaube, er teilte das Leben überhaupt nur nach Disziplin ein und Bewußtheit und historischer Notwendigkeit. Bei ihm war alles "klar" und "logisch" und "verständlich." Alles stimmte und war ganz einfach.
> Manchmal glaube ich nicht, daß alles so einfach ist und man nur die Ursachen und Anlässe zu finden braucht. (p. 36)

In the case of Tolja, the author also shows his inner problems and uncertainties. He shows how Tolja's desire to draw attention to himself, to be considered someone special, stems from his personal problems. "Er spielt den Hippie, den Clown im Hörsaal und wartet auf Beifall," observes Yana. "Wenn der ausbleibt, will er ihn erzwingen mit einem dreifachen Salto mortale" (p. 126). The author reveals a facet of his hero and heroine which is not solved by the collective alone, but which calls forth the responsibility of the private individual as well.

In the *Kurzgeschichte* "Die Waage,"[21] Günter Kunert goes a step further: he suggests that the individual does have a responsibility to the individual, which need not be identical with his responsibility to the collective. The hero, who wears a medal "für vorbildliche Planerfüllung" (p. 15), is devoted to progress and to his collective. As he is hurrying to take over his night shift, he accidentally collides with an old drunken man who appears suddenly and unexpectedly in front of him on the road, "um ihm den wichtigsten Weg zu verlegen: den zur Pflichterfüllung" (p. 18), as the author puts it. His desire to be on time for work, to put the interests of the collective first, becomes, at the same time, an excuse to flee the scene of the accident, and to evade his personal responsibility. Günter Kunert cryptically indicates the thinking behind his action: "Nutz oder nichtnutz, das war hier die Frage. Nützlich was für wen. Nicht umsonst gelernt. Alles im Zusammenhang sehen. Gelernt: Alles dialektisch betrachten. Gelernt: Einzelinteressen treten zurück . . ." (p. 21). The protagonist has learned that private interests are to give way to collective

---

[20] Plavius, "Gespräch mit Werner Heiduczek," p. 22.
[21] In *Die Beerdigung findet in aller Stille statt: Erzählungen,* Reihe Hanser, 11, 4th ed. (München: Hanser, 1970).

interests: however, as the author shows, he is still responsible for his action. In this *Kurzgeschichte,* Günter Kunert stresses the moral responsibility of the individual, who sometimes has to make his own crucial decisions outside the collective.

Irmtraud Morgner, in her story *Gauklerlegende: Eine Spielfraungeschichte,*[22] presents yet another aspect of the private individual, his imagination. She portrays two characters: Hubert, the scientist, and Wanda, the imaginative one, who opens herself up to an element of fantasy and makes friends with a mysterious juggler. When Irmtraud Morgner was asked in an interview whether in her stories the poetic imagination is seen in contrast to the scientific imagination, she observed: "Da ist kein Kontrapunkt im Sinne von Gegensatz, da sind zwei mögliche Seiten der Welterkenntnis."[23] Thus, she gives equal emphasis both to the scientific and the imaginative ways of looking at the world; she considers them to be complementary.

About her approach to literature, Irmtraud Morgner says: "Literarische Qualität ist für mich: größtmögliche Nähe des Autors zu sich selbst. Und: Menschenfreundlichkeit" (ibid., p. 1013). Thus self-awareness and consideration of others are essential for her. This is equally important to Christa Wolf, who once said in an interview: "Ich finde, es ist ein großer Gedanke, daß der Mensch nicht zur Ruhe kommt, ehe er zu sich selber gefunden hat . . ."[24] Although in most *Erzählungen* and *Kurzgeschichten* of the GDR, the usual problem is that of the individual's way into the collective, Christa Wolf does not regard this as the only possibility which an individual has to realize his full potential. Instead of being the goal of the development of the individual, the collective, in her view, is rather the means for a person to unfold his personality. She thus stresses,

> wie absurd die Meinung ist, daß die sozialistische Literatur sich nicht mit den feinen Nuancen des Gefühlslebens oder mit den individuellen Unterschieden der Charaktere befassen könne oder daß sie darauf angewiesen sei, Typen zu schaffen, die sich in vorgegebenen soziologischen Bahnen bewegen. Ich möchte geradezu sagen, im Gegenteil, wir gehen aus vom Recht des Individuums auf Selbstverwirklichung und machen uns daran, die realen Bedingungen dafür zu schaffen . . . (ibid.)

She emphasizes the inner life of the individual and, at the same time, places it within the context of socialist life. This, of course, could give rise to the question of how the various writers interpret socialism.

---

[22] Berlin: Eulenspiegel Verlag, 1970.
[23] Joachim Walther, "Autoren-Werkstatt: Irmtraud Morgner," *Weltbühne,* 47, 8 August 1972, 1012.
[24] "Christa Wolf liest aus 'Nachdenken über Christa T.': Zu Beginn ein Gespräch mit der Schriftstellerin über die Arbeit an der Erzählung," Berliner Rundfunk [Ost], 18 October 1966.

In her essay "Glauben an Irdisches," Christa Wolf comments about a statement made by Anna Seghers: "Alles hat sich im Innern der Menschen vollzogen."[25] She says: "Literatur, die aufhörte, den Wandlungen und Gefahren im Innern der Menschen nachzuspüren, würde ihrer Bestimmung untreu und verzichtete auf die Wirkungsmöglichkeit, die ihr und nur ihr vorbehalten ist."[26] Also, in her "Vorwort" to a collection of stories by Juri Kasakow, a modern Soviet writer, she underscores an observation which he makes: "Aber ich neige dazu, der Biographie des Innenlebens den Vorrang zu geben."[27] Thus, to her the reflective approach, which gives expression to the inner life of the individual, is vital. Rolf Floß, the author of the *Erzählung Irina*,[28] echoes this attitude, when he makes a distinction between two kinds of writers in the introductory remarks to his story:

> Die Frage nach literarischen Vorbildern zu beantworten fällt mir schwer, da diese sich mit mir verändern ... Christa Wolf wäre ... zu nennen, Jurij Kasakow und Hermann Kant. Auch von Schriftstellern beeinflussen mich die nachdenklichen mehr als die scheinbar so souveränen.[29]

However, the *Erzählungen* and *Kurzgeschichten* in which the individual is primarily significant as a private person are the exception; the narrative prose works of socialist realism emphasize the subordination of the individual to the collective, due to its major role in the new society. Most of the prose narratives investigated and mentioned in this chapter depict the model collective, the individual's choice to take the step "vom Ich zum Wir," and his responsibility towards the collective, which in turn cares for him. They also show the priority of the claims of the collective, which even supersede family ties, thus indicating the vital role of the collective in the life of the individual, as it is presented in the literature of the GDR.

---

[25] Seghers quoted by Christa Wolf, "Glauben an Irdisches," in *Lesen und Schreiben: Aufsätze und Betrachtungen*, Edition Neue Texte (Berlin: Aufbau-Verlag, 1972), p. 118.

[26] Wolf, "Glauben an Irdisches," p. 118.

[27] Kasakow quoted by Christa Wolf, "Vorwort," in *Larifari und andere Erzählungen* by Juri Kasakow (Berlin: Verlag Kultur und Fortschritt, 1967), p. 5.

[28] Halle/Saale: Mitteldeutscher Verlag, 1970.

[29] "Irina," *NDL*, 16, No. 9 (1968), 121–22.

Chapter III

THE THEME OF CHANGE

When in his "Thesen über Feuerbach," Karl Marx said, "Die Philosophen haben die Welt nur verschieden *interpretiert;* es kommt aber darauf an, sie zu *verändern,"*[1] he set a basis for socialist action. This ideal finds a prominent place in the literature of the GDR, in which the theme of changing the world around us is expressed and represented frequently and consistently. In his essay "Das neue Menschenbild: Wirklichkeit und Wirkung," Werner Neubert underscores this fact, when he observes:

> In den Feuerbach-Thesen erscheint der Mensch, das Individuum als das Ensemble der gesellschaftlichen Verhältnisse, als der Veränderer seiner Umwelt und seiner selbst. Und tatsächlich hat alle sozialistische Literatur, beginnend mit Weerths literarischer Skizze "Das Blumenfest der englischen Arbeiter" aus dem Jahre 1845, über Maxim Gorkis "Mutter" von 1906 bis hin zu unserer neuen Gegenwartsliteratur in der Deutschen Demokratischen Republik wesentlich die umgestaltende Kraft des Menschen, seine Fähigkeiten und Möglichkeiten gestaltet.[2]

Thus, again and again in the *Erzählungen* and *Kurzgeschichten* of the GDR, the struggle of the individual to achieve change in his society is depicted.

An indication of the importance of the theme of change is the frequent use of the terms "Anderswerden" and "Andersmachen," especially by the literary critics and theoreticians of the GDR. "Anderswerden" presupposes a change of attitude in the individual, and "Andersmachen" suggests that the man who has been changed in his attitude by socialist thought takes upon himself the task of changing the world around him. The concept of "Anderswerden" is a central motif in the works of Johannes R. Becher, who greatly influenced the writers of the GDR that came after him, as Hans Jürgen Geerdts observes: "Das große und zentrale Motiv des 'Anderswerdens' (Becher), das die älteren sozialistischen Schriftsteller immer wieder den neuen, veränderten sozialen Bedingungen entsprechend gestalteten, wurde von den jüngeren aufgenommen."[3] Also the literary critics of the GDR often use this concept and speak of the "Anderswerden der Menschen unter dem Einfluß der Revolution" (Pracht and Neubert, p. 83), "vom großen Anderswerden der Menschen" (ibid., p. 40), and of the "produktive Bereitschaft zum Andersmachen."[4] These two terms bring to the fore the dialectics of change: as the socialist consciousness of the

---

[1] Marx and Engels, *Werke* (Berlin: Dietz, 1959), III, 535.
[2] *NDL,* 16, No. 1 (1968), 4.
[3] "Einleitung," in *Literatur der DDR in Einzeldarstellungen,* p. XVII.
[4] Simons, " 'Das Andersmachen, von Grund auf,' " p. 195.

individual grows and develops, he himself is able to bring about change in the
world around him; he thus becomes both the object and the subject of change
in a socialist society.

The individual who brings about change

The chief characteristic of the leader in the new society, that is, the
individual who is ahead of the others in bringing about change, is that he is
"bewußt." A person who is "bewußt" is one who knows the ideology of
socialism and is committed to it; he is able to change himself and his society.
Pracht and Neubert speak of "dieser *wissende* Mensch" (p. 128), who, besides
possessing "schöpferische Initiative" (ibid.), also has "die Theorie vom Weg im
Kopf" (ibid.). The term "Wissen" is closely intertwined with this socialist
concept; for example, Pracht and Neubert mention that "Bewußtheit" is "das
Wissen um die gesamtgesellschaftlichen Entwicklungsgesetze . . ." (ibid.). The
men who have this knowledge form the vanguard of the socialist society and
are its pacemakers ("Schrittmacher"). They are the ones who embody the ideal
expressed in Marx's Eleventh Thesis on Feuerbach mentioned at the beginning
of this chapter. Pracht and Neubert state: "Im wissenden Menschen ist die
tätige Seite im Sinne der elften Feuerbach-These von Marx integriert" (ibid.).

In Helmut Sakowski's *Erzählung* "Zwei Zentner Leichtigkeit,"[5] the author
says about his character Fritz Dallmann, who has made a decision which is in
line with his socialist ideals: "Schließlich ist er seit siebenundvierzig Genosse
und kennt sich aus in der Klassenfrage" (p. 162). He implies that Fritz
Dallmann is *bewußt,* that he is well versed in socialist ideology, and is,
therefore, equipped to be a changer of society, as is amply shown in the
Erzählung.

Closely related to the term "bewußt" is the expression "selbstbewußt,"
used to indicate a characteristic of a member of a socialist society: his
self-confidence and self-reliance. Thus, Fritz Dallmann, the hero of Sakowski's
Erzählung, who by his example and leadership started a thriving LPG in his
village, speaks in a manner which is "selbstbewußt" (p. 176). In Werner
Bräunig's *Erzählung* "Gewöhnliche Leute," the author remarks about the
workers at the construction site: "Sie bewegen sich immer weiter hinaus in die
Umgebung. Wer wollte, konnte es den Leuten ansehen: Sie stiefelten mit einer
Selbstbewußtheit durchs Gelände . . ." (p. 26).

Sakowski's hero Fritz Dallmann is an example of the individual who
possesses these characteristics. At first, he hesitates to give up his own farm to
form a collective, but when he is reminded that "Genosse sein heißt Vorbild

---

[5] In *Zwei Zentner Leichtigkeit.*

sein" (p. 167), he takes the initiative and becomes the chairman of the struggling LPG. Building it up against great odds, he shows what an individual can do when he uses initiative and imagination. He also encourages the other people in the community to undertake the project of draining swampy land. In earlier times this suggestion would have been considered to be unrealistic, but now it becomes possible because of his example. Dallmann is a leader in his community, a man of quick wit and energy, who incorporates "das Selbstbewußtsein der Arbeiterklasse..." (Pracht and Neubert, p. 154). His high degree of socialist consciousness, and the force of his personality and sense of responsibility for others, enable him to stand at the forefront of socialist progress.

Arno Rettig, a character in Helmut Sakowski's "Wie sich das Nachdenken ausgezahlt hat," is a progressive individual, who, like Dallmann, has made a conscious choice for socialism and is a "Wissender," actively involved in initiating and encouraging change in his society. He realizes that in order to do so, his personal participation in the socialist reorganization of life in the GDR is necessary, and he does his share in building up the LPG in his village. Sakowski says about him: "Der Rettig hat so eine Maxime: Gegen den Strom schwimmen hat keinen Zweck, mit dem Strom schwimmen macht keinen Spaß, also setzt man sich an die Spitze. – So wird er Schrittmacher..." (p. 196).

Werner Konz, the Party secretary in Erik Neutsch's *Erzählung* "Drei Tage unseres Lebens," too, is a "Wissender" and a "Schrittmacher." He is fully aware of his responsibility in a socialist society, and is completely involved in his task of helping to modernize a town and in directing and guiding the town planners in this venture. Werner Bräunig's heroes Hannes Stütz in "Gewöhnliche Leute" and Peter Trumm in "Der schöne Monat August" also have a socialist consciousness, and they are exemplary individuals and leaders. Stütz takes the initiative in introducing better ways of working and in setting goals for the other workers at the construction site. Peter Trumm starts a community action which saves their excavation from a catastrophe. Their achievements point to the qualities which, according to Elisabeth Simons, the individual who brings about change in a socialist society possesses: "entwickelte Schöpferkraft und die höhere Bewußtseinsstufe der Werktätigen..."[6]

These *Erzählungen* portray this kind of leader; he is an individual with a well-developed socialist consciousness, who is *bewußt* and is able to recognize and to make use of all the opportunities for change that are available to him. These stories also emphasize the fact that it is through the individual that change comes about. According to Pracht and Neubert, this is a basic aspect of the literature of socialist realism:

[6] " 'Das Andersmachen, von Grund auf,' " p. 186.

Entscheidend für den sozialistischen Realismus ist, das "Schicksal" als Tätigkeit von Menschen, als Wirken — historisch konkret determinierbarer — sozialer Triebkräfte zu begreifen und somit als durch die eigene Tat veränderbar und beherrschbar darzustellen. (p. 133)

The teacher and mentor

The heroes of some of Benito Wogatzki's *Erzählungen* as, for example, "Ein Tag und eine Nacht" and "Der letzte Streich,"[7] possess not only a socialist consciousness, but also wisdom and much experience, and they play a fatherly role to some other individual. They are wise guides who are ahead of the others in maturity as members of the new society. They help to bring about change, not only in the area of technology and economic production, but also in the lives and attitudes of men.

In Benito Wogatzki's *Erzählung* "Der letzte Streich," Papa Kolbe is the mentor and counselor to Schemmel, who, bankrupt in every way, begins work as a scrubber of vats in a textile plant in which Papa Kolbe holds a position of responsibility. Through his influence and example, Schemmel becomes a leader and pacemaker himself, who in turn is able to lead and guide other workers. One of these is Bertram, also a scrubber of vats, who, through Schemmel's help and encouragement, eventually rises to become a member of his mentor's research team.

Similarly, the brigadier in Benito Wogatzki's "Ein Tag und eine Nacht" plays a fatherly role to Ham, the truckdriver in his work gang, to his wife Ursula, and to Willi, a fellow caterpillar operator. He becomes involved in their personal lives: he listens to Ursula's story, takes care of her little boy, helps Willi to gain insight into his actions and attitudes and his responsibility to his fellow workers, and saves Ham's marriage. His concern is to make sure that the all-important "Zyklogramm" will not be disrupted by disharmonies in the personal relationships of his workers.

A similar theme about the change brought about in an individual's life by the fatherly guidance and help of a person who is more advanced and has a well-developed socialist consciousness is found in the *Kurzgeschichte* "Die Ansprache"[8] by Siegfried Pitschmann. The protagonist Matschoß stays at home alone on the day of his friend's funeral and recalls the times they had together. In expressing his grief, he speaks to his friend as if he were still present; his words reveal the significance of the man's friendship in his life:

---

[7] In *Der Preis des Mädchens.*
[8] In *Kontrapunkte.*

Vorher war ich ja nur'n Klumpen Lehm, kaum zu gebrauchen, und du hast mir Leben eingeblasen, und jetzt renne ich wahrhaftig herum wie'n Halber Hahn und weiß nicht, was ich machen soll ohne dich ... und wenn ich dich mal sehen will, muß ich ins Verwaltungshaus und mit Passierschein in den Flügel, der Partei ist, wo das schöne Malerbild von dir hängt. (pp. 116–17)

His reference to the portrait of his friend suggests that he was a man who had distinguished himself as a socialist and worker. Matschoß, however, had a humble post as a watchman at a cement factory when they first met. He says about the man who befriended and helped him: "Immer wie'n Mensch zu mir, wo früher kaum einer hingesehen hat, daß ich noch am Leben war. . . . Und niemals dieses Gönnergetue, wenn du helfen wolltest . . ." (p. 115). The man lives with Matschoß in the same workers' quarters, and he encourages him to improve himself. For example, Matschoß has to read the paper:

Hatte ich jeden Tag zu üben, da warst du eisern, erstens wegen Lesen, zweitens wegen Horizont und Polit, und drittens wegen Stottern. Früher kriegte ich ja keinen Satz raus, ohne zu spucken und zu schnattern, und du hast erklärt, daß es von der langen Angst kam, vom Anfang im Findelheim . . . (pp. 111–12)

Later, he helps Matschoß find a wife, and when there is no money for furniture, he persuades him to improve his qualifications for a better job, and, furthermore, helps him to stick to his plan until his goal has been achieved. "Was du gemacht hast; 'n schweres Programm, 'n schweres Programm, 'n halbes Plenum, aber wir haben es geschafft" (p. 116), declares Matschoß.

In Benito Wogatzki's *Erzählungen,* the figure of the wise teacher is somewhat aloof and stereotyped, of someone who is always successful and optimistic, but Siegfried Pitschmann manages to convey a relationship based on a genuine friendship, in which both have good times together, even though one is a socialist hero, and the other a man who is at first a wretched and isolated individual. Matschoß says of his friend: "Du hast schon gewußt, welche Spritze richtig war für mich" (p. 111). Moreover, their relationship is more than that of a wise teacher helping someone; it is also a personal encounter in which one man gives of himself as a person. In this *Kurzgeschichte,* Pitschmann depicts an ideal socialist relationship between a mentor and his charge.

The naive socialist

In some *Erzählungen,* the individuals who bring about change are presented as naive socialists who seemingly do what is right instinctively, because they are good-hearted and want to help their fellow men. The authors do not suggest how they have acquired their socialist consciousness; simply by their actions they reveal their right attitude. This seems to indicate that a socialist

consciousness is something so essentially human that it can develop spontaneously in a person who is naive, that is, whose consciousness has not been
corrupted by his education and his experiences. These men are usually not in
positions of responsibility, but are rather obscure and simple citizens, who see
that something can, or should, be done to bring about improvements, and who
do something about it. In the stories to be discussed under this aspect, three
such characters are unpretentious and rather obscure old men, simple and
honest workers, who can see what is wrong and who act accordingly. One is a
teen-age girl, who, to achieve an improvement for her village, is unsuccessful in
convincing the men in positions of authority, who ought to be the ones with a
well-developed socialist consciousness, and has to turn to an old carpenter for
aid.

The hero of Joachim Nowotny's story "Julius auf dem Baume"[9] is an old
man who cannot help speaking out when he sees something wrong. Three times
Julius has disrupted the plans of others, and also got himself into trouble, by
speaking his mind at meetings of the local LPG. For example, he persuades the
others to give a delinquent girl a second chance by providing her with some
responsibility in the LPG, and he takes upon himself the risk if it does not
work out. Unfortunately, she runs away after three weeks. After this fiasco, he
hides in a tree to avoid going to another meeting, for, as he says, all he has to
do is sit at the meeting and he disrupts it: "Hab' da einen verdammt komischen
Charakter, nicht wahr, kann die Weltgeschichte einfach nicht so laufen lassen
wie sie läuft. Hau' mich da immer zwischen" (pp. 151–52). Therefore he says
he cannot go. However, the author suggests that it is precisely his penchant for
making others uncomfortable with the usual ways of doing things and for
offering other ideas that makes him a valuable member of the new society.
Julius' actions are consonant with the ideals of socialism and inadvertently he
ends up being the progressive one. Thus, in a humorous manner, Joachim
Nowotny portrays a modern pacemaker who, however, is ironically unaware of
being one.

In Volker Braun's *Erzählung Das ungezwungne Leben Kasts,* a minor
character, a patient in the hospital in which the hero finds himself, is a man
who is full of hope for the changes that he sees coming and, in his own way,
does what he can in helping to change the world around him. A humble old
mechanic, he reminds other workers that the scrap iron they are wasting at
their place of work is their own money. He exhorts Kast:

Sieh zu, daß du das Neue siehst. Das ist das, was die Leute selbst wollen, immer mehr.
Nur traun sie sichs oft nicht zu, weil sie glauben, sie sind nichts. Weil das Neue immer
von woanders kam und aufgezwungen. Jetzt solls von ihnen kommen. . . . Wir sind

---

[9]   In *Labyrinth ohne Schrecken.*

schon so weit, daß wir beim Arbeiten Helden werden können. Wir müssen so weit kommen, daß wir es nicht mehr werden können – daß wir immer so sind . . . (p. 38)

This old worker emphasizes the fact that change and social improvements should come from the lower ranks, that it should come spontaneously from them, he himself being an example of this.

Similarly, in Helmut Sakowski's story "Schlechte Zeiten für die Mäuse,"[10] an obscure member of a small village achieves prominence by writing a letter to the newspaper telling the truth about the plight of their neglected LPG. In this way, old Herbert Middelstädt is able to bring about a change in the fortunes of the village collective: "Da hat einer ausgesprochen, was viele dachten. Da hat einer genau ins Schwarze getroffen. Und nun tut sich was in Grünow" (p. 148). He has had the courage to tell of the mismanagement which he saw, and this led to a wave of improvements; he had, as the author says, "den Stein ins träge, stehende Wasser geworfen, nun wachsen die Ringe immer größer" (ibid.). The author emphasizes the fact that an old obscure grandfather achieves unexpected fame and success by doing "was selbstverständlich ist" (ibid.).

In his story "Podelziger Intermezzo,"[11] Joachim Nowotny again presents a rather unlikely candidate for a changer of society. A sixteen-year-old girl has her heart set on having a stream and a swampy meadow converted into a pond for her town, and she uses her imagination and persistence to achieve this goal, thus creating something practical and beautiful for others. She approaches three different people, who should be leaders of social change, with her plan, but none of them takes her seriously; they do not wish to be disturbed and are too busy. Finally, she is able to persuade an old carpenter to help her. Afterwards, everybody is convinced and grateful. The author comments:

Drei vernünftige und im großen und ganzen geachtete Leute haben die Idee eines kleinen Mädchens für Humbug gehalten, weil sie ihnen nicht in den Kram paßte. Der eine wollte seine Ruhe haben, der andere protzte ein bischen mit dem neuen Wort Melioration, und der dritte schließlich erboste sich darüber, daß ihm da jemand ins Handwerk pfuschte. . . . jeder dachte: Wie kann das gut sein, was aus dem Kopf eines sechzehnjährigen Dinges stammt? (pp. 264–65)

The individuals portrayed in the above-mentioned stories are progressive and help to change the world around them; however, their "schöpferische Initiative" (p. 128), as it is called by Pracht and Neubert, springs spontaneously from their heart and they know instinctively what should be done. They demonstrate that it is not the position or office an individual may hold in a socialist society that is important, but rather taking the initiative and beginning

[10] In *Zwei Zentner Leichtigkeit.*
[11] In *Labyrinth ohne Schrecken.*

to change what needs to be changed. In his *Erzählung* "Schlechte Zeiten für die Mäuse," Helmut Sakowski comments about his character Herbert Middelstädt, the old grandfather who dares to take the necessary steps to improve the LPG of his village: "Und der Mensch soll sich was zutrauen. Und warum soll er sich nicht hochschätzen, wenn er erkennt, daß er die Kraft hat, seine Welt zu verändern? " (p. 148).

The converted socialist

Erwin Strittmatter's *Erzählung* "Bedenkzeit"[12] suggests another variation of the theme of change and the relationships of the individual in a socialist society. Eddie Kienast, the protagonist, has to change his attitude before he can contribute in a positive way to his society. He undergoes a process of "Anderswerden": his oldfashioned, obsolete ideas and narrow horizon, in which his self-importance loomed large, give way to a progressive outlook consonant with socialist ideals.

At first, Kienast, as the hard-working chairman of a successful LPG, is an example to the others. However, he looks at the thriving collective farm as the fruit of his own efforts and ability, not giving credit where it is due. When a neighbouring village wants to join, he refuses, and thus shows how closed he is to progress and change, merely wanting to maintain the *status quo*. When Kienast is demoted and replaced by Glante, he sulks and refuses to have anything to do with the new leadership of the LPG. "Haß verfälschte mir den Blick . . . ," he admits. "Ich lauerte gierig auf Glantes großen Fehler, für den man ihn stürzen würde, wie man mich gestürzt hatte" (p. 235). He withdraws to live a private life, reading and wondering about the meaning of life, and does his work as an ordinary farmer in the LPG.

However, Glante needs his help in his plan to build a new barn for raising pigs, and he asks Kienast to take a course in hog-raising. Kienast is offended since he considers himself to be an expert in this area, until he visits another LPG which has an ultra-modern barn. He is so impressed with the efficient and highly mechanized building that he realizes he must overcome his rivalry and dislike of Glante to warn him that his plans for the barn may already be obsolete. Moreover, he decides to take a course in electricity as his contribution to the modern barn that he envisions on their own LPG.

The new society has opened his eyes, and Eddie Kienast undergoes a process of "Anderswerden" by making the decision to serve and to participate in it. He is then able to help in the process of "Andersmachen" by showing Glante the new possibilities of building a better and more modern barn. Thus,

---

[12] In *Ein Dienstag im September.*

he shares his new-found knowledge and vision, co-operates with his former rival, learns new skills and in these ways shows the development of his socialist consciousness. He is now able to fit into the new LPG and to contribute to it in a helpful and positive way.

The dreamer and man of vision

Another individual who brings about change in a socialist society is the dreamer, the man who is capable of *vorwärtsträumen*, of seeing the present in terms of the ideal future as it is envisioned in socialism. To him, the quality of "dreaming ahead," "jenes 'Träumens nach vorn,' von dem Impulse zur Veränderung der Wirklichkeit ausgehen, weil es die Bereitschaft weckt, die Vorstellung von einem schöneren, erfüllten menschlichen Leben ins Heute zu zwingen" (Pracht and Neubert, p. 158), is essential. The individual who is filled with this dream is able to initiate change. The figure of Wandeck, the construction engineer in Benito Wogatzki's *Erzählung* "Ein Tag und eine Nacht," is such a dreamer. He needs big ideas: "Ihm gingen fast immer große Gedanken durch den Kopf. Meistens dann, wenn andere über den Schlamassel zeterten und ihre Zigaretten wütend in die Erde traten" (p. 374); "Er klammerte sich ununterbrochen an große Gedanken" (p. 376). He becomes excited about possible human accomplishments, about machines, about the future. He exclaims: "Heute findet das Zusammenspiel der verschiedensten Fähigkeiten auf ganz neuer Stufe statt . . . Begreife das mal, daß ausgerechnet du an der Reihe bist, die Jahrhunderte in ein vernünftiges System zu bringen. Schwindelig kann einem werden!" (p. 375).

These leaders of change awaken enthusiasm in others and sweep them along. Hannes Stütz, the hero of Werner Bräunig's "Gewöhnliche Leute" is such a man. Because of his courageous and forward looking leadership, he makes it possible for others to move ahead more rapidly, too: "Es gab welche, die kamen da nicht mehr mit, aber es gab hauptsächlich andere, die jetzt erst richtig zum Zug kamen" (p. 53). Kast, in Volker Braun's *Erzählung Das ungezwungne Leben Kasts,* is also conscious of this quality in a person; he observes: "Und der einzelne, sei er noch so ein Bahnbrecher – [ist] erst wichtig, wenn er viele mitreißt" (p. 111). He sees this forward motion as essential for the progress of society: "Was uns allenfalls fehle," he suggests, "seien große Unternehmungen der Gesellschaft, jedenfalls so große, daß sie uns aus uns selber reißen!" (p. 75).

Erik Neutsch's *Erzählung* "Drei Tage unseres Lebens" also portrays a man of vision. Konz, the Party secretary, is ahead of the others in his daring plans and thinks in terms of the future. "Ja, er hatte den Mond vom Himmel heruntergeholt. Die Saale floß schon bergauf. So also sah er die Rekonstruktion unserer Stadt. In diesen Größen dachte er" (p. 167), observes Brüdering, the

mayor of the town Konz wants to change, after one of the Party secretary's
speeches to the town-planning committee. Later in the story, when Brüdering
and Konz visit the home of the streetcar conductor and discuss the new plan
for the town with the family, the mayor comments: "Konz schlug wieder
Brücken zum Mond. Sprach er von einem Tunnel, so meinte er Raumfahrt, und
er zwang auch die Frauen zum Nachdenken" (p. 197). Thus, he even draws
others along to share his vision.

    Such a man is needed to take the first step in initiating something new.
"Bedurfte es wirklich erst eines Mannes wie Konz? " (p. 189), wonders
Brüdering. When Konz and Koblenz arrive at a satisfactory plan, and the Party
secretary asks Koblenz why he has not presented his suggestions earlier, he
replies: "Vorher war wohl die Zeit nicht danach. Oder es fehlte am Geld. Oder
es fehlte das Material. Vielleicht aber fehlte nur einer, der in Dimensionen
dachte wie Sie . . ." (ibid.).

    In Benito Wogatzki's *Erzählung* "Der letzte Streich," the hero, Schemmel,
is a dreamer and discoverer of new things. Kolbe says of him: "Kennt man ja
. . . was so ein richtig lebendiger Mensch ist, der hat die Phantasie in den
Fingern, der macht aus allem was . . . Der muß eben fummeln und zaubern"
(p. 64). Dr. Alexander, in the same *Erzählung,* is also such a man of unlimited
ideas: "Einmal war das so einer, der zum Neuen neigte, der sozusagen ständig
der Verlockung unterlag, was Neues anzuschieben. Schemmel mit seinen Ideen
fand . . . stets einen Enthusiasten, der alles bereits vor sich sah, und das Größte
zuerst" (p. 70).

    Benito Wogatzki suggests that, to be truly effective in his efforts to bring
about change, the dreamer needs someone to complement his creativity and to
provide a balance for him, so that his ideas do not become unrealistic. Thus,
the effectiveness of Dr. Alexander's contribution becomes possible only as he
works together with his deputy, Genosse Hauser. Whereas Dr. Alexander
"schob eben immer nur an. Er war so mehr ein Ideenproduzent . . ." (ibid.),
Genosse Hauser tests everything, and only when the practical difficulties have
been removed, does he go ahead. Together they make up an effective team: "Ja
fast ist man geneigt anzunehmen, daß gerade aus dem Kampf dieser beiden Pole
die besten Sachen hervorgingen. Der eine sorgte dafür, daß die neuen Ideen am
Kochen blieben — der andere für die Grundlagen ihrer Verwirklichung" (p. 71).

    Similarly, Erik Neutsch, in the *Erzählung* "Drei Tage unseres Lebens,"
shows that Konz needs the wisdom and concern of Brüdering, who has many
years of experience in dealing with the people of the town, so that he will not
lose sight of the human side in the race for technological advance. Brüdering
reminds Konz: "Vergiß nicht bei all deinen Zukunftsträumen, deine Gedanken,
deine stahlgrauen Augen auf die Gegenwart zu richten. Wenn du die Stadt
ändern willst, denke an ihre Menschen" (p. 141).

The human side of technological progress

An aspect of the theme of change which recurs in *Erzählungen* and *Kurzgeschichten* of the GDR is that the human element has to be taken into consideration in the midst of rapid technological advance. Uninhibited progress and human life are sometimes at odds, and thus, the process of change has to be modified. In his *Erzählung* "Drei Tage unseres Lebens," Erik Neutsch suggests the inhuman way in which a town may be sacrificed to the interests of technology; his character Mayor Brüdering observes:

> Sie verhandelten über die Stadt, sie verschacherten sie, als sei es ein toter Gegenstand, als lebten darin nicht zweihunderttausend Menschen. Ich wollte fragen: Wenn ihr die Stadt versenkt, tief in die Erde hinein, wenn ihr sie aufbaut oder zerstört, was auf dasselbe hinausläuft, wohin schüttet ihr dann ihren Inhalt? An den Häusern hängen Familien. Jeder Stein hat seine Geschichte. (p. 188)

Brüdering is concerned about the people. The human element must not be lost sight of in the sometimes ruthless striving for change and progress.

In Volker Braun's *Erzählung Das ungezwungne Leben Kasts,* the protagonist is also concerned about the individual in times of rapid progress. Kast writes in a letter to Linde: "Diese Zeit bricht soviel um in der Wirklichkeit und an Verhaltensnormen, und baut soviel anderes auf, daß es Mühe kostet, nichts am einzelnen Menschen zu zerbrechen" (p. 79). The impact of unlimited progress and technological change can be a heavy burden on the individual. This situation is evident, for example, in Bernd Jentzsch's *Kurzgeschichte* "Josefski,"[13] where the old man, who has always served the socialist cause devotedly, finds himself suddenly and ironically swept aside by the rapid progress for which he has striven, and he has to be replaced by a man with a better technical education.

The suggestion, that problems may result if technological change occurs too quickly and the human being is ignored, is also made in Benito Wogatzki's *Erzählung* "Der Preis des Mädchens." Jochen Möllenthin is interested in improving and changing the means of production in an industrial plant as quickly and efficiently as possible, but, in doing so, he does not take into consideration the people who operate them. The director of the plant, in trying to remind him that he is dealing with human beings, not only machines, takes him to the assembly line to meet the actual workers. When Möllenthin falls in love with one of the girls there, his personal experience helps him to realize that his understanding of life and reality is limited, and that he will have to change his attitude to include other values than just those of efficiency and a high rate of production.

---

[13] In *Neunzehn Erzähler der DDR*, ed. Hans-Jürgen Schmitt.

A different aspect of the role of the human being in the technological developments of the new society is presented in the *Erzählung* "Ein Tag und eine Nacht" by Benito Wogatzki. Technological centralization and specialization, as symbolized by the "Zyklogramm," largely set the tone in this story. The brigadier is aware that since technology is undergoing continual change ("Chemieverfahren altern schneller als Jungfrauen . . ." [p. 368]), and that the means of production are developing at a rapid rate, then the individual, too, has to change in his attitudes to be able to fit in. He has to have a good relationship with his fellow workers, if the work processes, the so-called "Zyklogramm," are to run smoothly. Anything that may cause friction in human relationships has to be avoided. Therefore, Willi, for example, has to be shown that he must look beyond his selfish interests and that he has a responsibility to others. According to Benito Wogatzki's *Erzählung,* the human being must change, too, to keep up with the progress made in the creation of more efficient ways of production.

The means of change

The concept of "nichtantagonistischer Widerspruch"[14] is presented as a basis for achieving social change in Erik Neutsch's *Erzählung* "Drei Tage unseres Lebens." The man who is ahead of the others in his socialist consciousness, and who has a task to perform involving change on a large scale, often causes a conflict, as in the case of the Party secretary Konz, who comes to a town which he has to help modernize. He has to carry out his purpose: "Er hatte den Auftrag zu siegen. Er verfocht den Generalverkehrsplan, und . . . für ihn gab es keine andere Möglichkeit, kein Zurück, nur das eine: zu siegen" (p. 169). However, when Konz is confronted with an alternative plan by his opponent, the chief architect Koblenz, he is willing to listen and to consider the plan carefully; he realizes that Koblenz' contribution, too, is vital. Since both men are members of a socialist society and Party members, they are on the same road, and, therefore, as in all non-antagonistic conflicts, "nicht mehr . . . unversöhnliche Partner" (Pracht and Neubert, p. 211). Their conflict is resolved by talking it out, and together, they are able to arrive at a superior plan. Thus, their conflict is the starting point and the propelling force in their endeavour to find the best solution possible.

Another means of encouraging and initiating change is depicted in Benito Wogatzki's *Erzählung* "Der letzte Streich." The leader who has to find ways of improving or starting new methods of production at an industrial plant turns to all the workers, inviting them to pool their ideas. The protagonist Schemmel is a master at using this method, having learned it from his predecessor Kolbe:

---

[14]   Helga Herting, *Das sozialistische Menschenbild in der Gegenwartsliteratur*, p. 66.

Da setzt er sich also hin und macht seinen Plan zurecht. Früh um sechs weiß er, was er will, und ruft die Leute zusammen. Was macht er nun? Er stellt sich dumm und wirft, von tiefer Sorge erfüllt, ein Problem auf. Nun luchst er, schaut in die Gesichter, wartet. Kommen lassen! Immer erst kommen lassen! (p. 63)

The people feel that they have a contribution to make, and, as they pool their ideas, many useful insights are gained, which no single individual, not even Schemmel, could have arrived at by himself. The author comments: "Am Ende jedenfalls ist jeder aus der Brigade fest davon überzeugt, daß er nun eigentlich nichts anderes zu tun hat, als seine eigenen schönen Gedanken in die Veränderung des irdischen Daseins einfließen zu lassen" (ibid.).

Furthermore, Schemmel has devised what he calls his "Spinnbuch" (p. 66), a thick book into which the workers can write any suggestions for change and improvement that may occur to them. The book is based on the idea, "daß nichts unwichtig ist und jede Verrücktheit erlaubt ist" (ibid.).

In many *Erzählungen* and *Kurzgeschichten* of the GDR, education is presented as an important avenue to change. The motif of education and study occurs again and again. In Volker Braun's *Erzählung Das ungezwungne Leben Kasts,* the hero exclaims:

Was kann ich machen? Es ist unvorstellbar, wie wir uns verhalten würden, wenn alles aus dem Überfluß geschähe. Wie sich alle Anschauungen und Gewohnheiten verkehrten zu etwas Unerhörtem, Einfachem! Wie sich die Produktion veränderte zu einem unerhörten Prozeß der Taten und Erfindungen, zu einer Kunst! – Aber wie kann es zu einem Überfluß an Gütern kommen, wenn wir uns zu Tausenden in die alten kleinen Tätigkeiten begeben, als wenn sie natürlich wären? (p. 41)

His companion answers him: "Wenn du die Technologie umwälzen willst, das meinst du wohl? , mußt du studieren" (ibid.).

Rita, in Benito Wogatzki's *Erzählung* "Der Preis des Mädchens," goes to night school and plans to go to university. In "Der letzte Streich" by the same author, Schemmel, beginning as a scrubber of vats, improves his qualifications by means of evening courses: "Schemmel absolvierte . . . den Meisterlehrgang. Neben der Arbeit natürlich und an den schichtfreien Tagen" (p. 56). In Helmut Sakowski's story "Die Aussteuer,"[15] a modern woman's best dowry is her education. In the *Kurzgeschichte* "Josefski" by Bernd Jentzsch, the protagonist's lack of education has tragic consequences for him; he is thwarted in his desire to contribute to the rapid technological changes occurring around him. Josefski has to step down from his post in favour of another man, who has training in computer science.

Three *Erzählungen* by Erwin Strittmatter contain the motif of studying; in each of them, it expresses the positive change in attitude which an individual

[15] In *Zwei Zentner Leichtigkeit.*

undergoes as a result of his studies. Furthermore, the protagonist's ability to break away from old ways of thinking by means of his newly acquired education is shown. Eddie Kienast, in "Bedenkzeit," makes the decision to become an electrician in order to be able to service the completely mechanized barn to be built on their LPG. His decision marks a profound change in his attitude to living progressively according to socialist ideals. At the end of the story, the author suggests that Kienast may continue his training and education in other areas as well.

The *Erzählung* "Der Stein"[16] by the same author demonstrates that the protagonist Werner Wurzel is a superior young farmer because he attends the *Bauernakademie.* His newly acquired knowledge and insight enable him to break away from a superstition, which his ancestors accepted about a stretch of land which had once belonged to them. Wurzel, as he is ploughing it for the LPG, investigates it, because he knows, "daß man die Behauptung seines Großvaters in neuerer Zeit durch neuere Behauptungen widerlegt hat . . ." (p. 222). Whereas for generations nothing had been done about the mysterious "Brandstelle" in the field, because of the superstition attached to it, Wurzel does not hesitate to change that which earlier generations had not questioned. He finds a huge stone under the surface, removes it with his tractor, and places it in the ditch, where it becomes a monument and symbol of an enlightened way of thinking, which is the result of education; Strittmatter calls the stone a "Denkmal eigener Art" (p. 229).

In Erwin Strittmatter's story "Ein Dienstag im September,"[17] Werner Wurzel explains why he plans to take some correspondence courses. The point made in this humorously told narrative is that Wurzel knows facts that he has learned at the *Bauernakademie,* which give him a distinct advantage over the other farmers in knowing how to handle a particular horse at the fair; when all the others make fools of themselves, he emerges as the hero of the day. Thus, as shown in the above-mentioned stories, education is important in every walk of life for the individual who wants to be a progressive member of a socialist society and to improve the conditions around him.

The concept of "das Mögliche"

In a number of *Erzählungen,* the concept of "das Mögliche" occurs in connection with the theme of change. This notion of the possible suggests that there is room for the individual's own decision and choice within the forward movement of socialist progress. In the span between possibility and necessity

---

[16]   In *Ein Dienstag im September.*
[17]   In *Ein Dienstag im September.*

lies his moral choice to act and to prove himself. In making full use of "das Mögliche," he can further his own socialist development and that of his society.

In Werner Bräunig's story "Gewöhnliche Leute," Adele Noth says about her own life and education: "Es war nicht immer leicht gewesen, manchmal schwer, manchmal unnötig schwer. Aber es war gut. Es war das Mögliche" (p. 45) She has made use of her opportunities to learn and to act and has become a successful member of the new society.

In the *Erzählung* "Der schöne Monat August" by the same author, the protagonist Peter Trumm observes that each individual is confronted by several possibilities of action. He ponders the problem: "Wir haben immer verschiedene Möglichkeiten, also müssen wir uns entscheiden, sonst kommt nichts dabei heraus, und wir müssen nach Möglichkeit richtig entscheiden oder wenigstens so gut als möglich . . ." (p. 126). Trumm emphasizes another aspect of the concept of "das Mögliche": the necessity of choice and the accompanying responsibility. He concludes that the essential thing is what the individual decides to do with what is possible: "Hauptsächlich liegt es an uns. Vielleicht geht es überhaupt immer bloß um die Spanne zwischen dem, was ist, und dem, was möglich ist, wenn wir ernsthaft etwas tun" (ibid.). Thus, Trumm puts the individual into the centre and places the responsibility for action upon him.

In Volker Braun's *Erzählung Das ungezwungne Leben Kasts,* the protagonist realizes, as he sets out in life, that the use of the possibilities set before him will depend upon him; he observes: "Hier war das Land, es war eine große Zeit, und das Mindeste, das ich von mir erwartete, war, ihre Möglichkeiten zu nutzen" (p. 25). In the same *Erzählung,* the old mechanic is optimistic and full of enterprise, knowing that many possibilities for achievement and change confront each individual. He exclaims: "Das sind erst Anfänge. Was wird alles sein! Was wird alles möglich sein! Es liegt an uns" (p. 37).

The Party secretary Werner Konz, in Erik Neutsch's *Erzählung* "Drei Tage unseres Lebens," suggests, in a speech to his collective, some far-fetched inventions and changes that may one day become a reality; he reminds his listeners: "Sagen wir nicht: Utopisch, das geht nicht. Fragen wir lieber, was notwendig ist, was getan werden muß, damit es getan werden kann. An die Arbeit. Suchen wir nach Möglichkeiten, um das Unmögliche möglich zu machen" (p. 164). He suggests another aspect of "das Mögliche." Not only is the individual to use the possibilities set before him, but also to seek ways, together with the other members of his collective, to attain goals which at first may appear impossible.

Hannes Stütz, the construction engineer in Bräunig's "Gewöhnliche Leute," makes the daring decision to finish the building of a high-rise apartment a hundred and twenty days ahead of schedule. Through the determination and resolute effort of Stütz and his co-workers, the seemingly impossible is achieved. The author comments: "Sie hatten angefangen mit dem Möglichen, dann hatten sie das scheinbar Unmögliche möglich gemacht" (p. 25).

The construction engineer Stütz, the Party secretary Konz, as well as Kast, all know that they need the support of the collective to accomplish the changes and improvements that will advance their society. Nevertheless, in the above references to "das Mögliche" in the *Erzählungen,* the choice and responsibility of the individual are emphasized. Social and technological change has to come about through the efforts of an individual who is *bewußt* and who is, thus, striving to realize his socialist ideals and the goals of the new society. He is the "Schrittmacher," confident and optimistic; Pracht and Neubert comment: "Prototyp geschichtlicher Veränderungen in der DDR ist bereits ein Mensch, der nicht allein die Schale des Mißtrauens in die eigene Kraft durchbrochen hat, sondern sich dieser Kraft in hohem Maße bewußt ist" (p. 128). He takes the initiative and acts within the realm of "das Mögliche"; in doing so, he energizes and inspires his collective as well, so that together they are able to accomplish what appears impossible.

At the same time, this person, who is a "Wissender," that is, one who is committed to socialism, is fully integrated with the collective, making its interests, and those of the socialist society, his own. His choice and responsibility within the span of possibility and necessity are guided and directed by socialist ideals and aims.

B. Types and Situations

Chapter IV
WOMEN IN THE NEW SOCIETY

In consonance with the principles of Marxism-Leninism, the new role of women is emphasized in socialist society. As a result, the literature of socialist realism frequently depicts some aspect of the emancipation of women or *Gleichberechtigung*. In a number of short prose narratives of the GDR, the motif of the equality of the rights of women is the central theme; in a number of others, it constitutes one of the aspects of the plot; and in some stories, a statement about *Gleichberechtigung* is voiced directly by one of the characters.

Because the contrast between the bourgeois attitudes of the past and the changes found in the new society is most dramatic in the case of the social role of women, the theme of *Gleichberechtigung* is popular among writers. Helmut Sakowski, when he was asked in an interview, why women play such a predominant role in his stories, observed:

> Die Frauen spielen im Leben – im persönlichen und gesellschaftlichen – eine große Rolle. Warum sollte man sie ausklammern aus der Literatur? Und außerdem glaube ich, daß man an der Geschichte von Frauen besonders deutlich machen kann, was charakteristisch ist für die Zeit, in der wir leben. Wenn man erzählt, welch große Entwicklung die Frauen bei uns durchgemacht haben, kann man einleuchtend und überzeugungskräftig beweisen, was sozialistische Gegenwart ist. Jeder Schriftsteller will originelle und interessante Geschichten erzählen, und derjenige Schriftsteller ist nicht klug, der sich diese Möglichkeit entgehen läßt.[1]

He points out that stories about women shed light on the relationship of the individual to the new society from an angle which shows most dramatically, with a maximum amount of contrast, the shift from traditional ways of thinking to those which characterize socialism. These stories can show especially clearly what is characteristic of the times and of the new society.

Aside from the ideological importance of the theme of *Gleichberechtigung* and the fact that it allows the writer to present the new society favourably, it contains some of the ingredients of a popular story. A pretty and charming heroine struggles courageously against great odds, including the backwardness of a husband or lover. A love story is often presented, in which there is usually scope for pathos and a human touch, thus making the narrative more appealing to the average reader.

In the various *Erzählungen* of the GDR which deal with the theme of the emancipated woman, the heroine is presented as an individual who is ahead of her times and the attitudes of those around her. She is an individual who is a

---

[1] Volker Kurzweg, "Interview mit Helmut Sakowski," *WB*, 15, No. 4 (1969), 750.

pacemaker, and she has a well-developed socialist consciousness. She is, above all, "eine bewußte Frau," who incorporates the socialist ideal. Her traditional role of wife and mother is usually superseded by her career. She often has a scientific career, or one previously associated with men, as, for example, a mechanic who repairs agricultural machinery, like the heroine of Werner Bräunig's "Die einfachste Sache der Welt," or a designer of machines, like Nora in "Akte Nora S." by Erik Neutsch. She is usually trying to improve her qualifications in order to rise to a higher position. She is presented as always being successful in her work, though in her personal life she may sometimes suffer a disappointment.

This new role of the woman depicts most dramatically the relationship of the individual to society. She stands out as the progressive individual, and, in contrast, any remnants of bourgeois thinking in the minds of others, usually the men in her life, are exposed.

The most popular area depicted in the short prose narratives in connection with the new role of women in socialist society is that of work. Her relationship with others in the collective of workers, the significance of her work in her life, and the conflict which often arises between her career and the selfish demands of a husband or lover, are shown. The woman's relationship in marriage and in love is another area in which her new role is explored. In some stories, the crisis situation, which arises when the lover or husband does not consider the woman as a person in her own right, is portrayed. Sometimes the woman herself has to make a positive choice for the new society; however, almost always it is the husband or lover who has to change. Even in stories in which *Gleichberechtigung* is not the obvious theme, the woman is usually portrayed as the more progressive individual and as having a better developed socialist consciousness than the man.

The conflict between a career and love

In a number of *Erzählungen*, the woman is caught in a conflict between her ambition and her career and the selfish demands of the man she loves. In Werner Heiduczek's *Erzählung Mark Aurel oder ein Semester Zärtlichkeit*, the situation of conflict which is presented is that of Yana's mother, who in her youth wanted to become an actress, but was prevented by her fiancé. Yana recounts: "Meine Mutter erzählte mir damals ihre Geschichte mit dem Vater und der Schauspielschule .... Ich hatte den Eindruck, als wenn sie nachträglich um sich selbst kämpfte" (p. 56). In her mother this was an unresolved conflict, because Yana's father had persisted in his selfish demand, and she had had to become a teacher instead, for, as Yana observes: "Er hatte sie vor die Wahl gestellt: Ich oder die Theaterhochschule" (p. 53). Yana probes this matter further and asks her father, who feels guilty, about it. She tells him:

"Wahrscheinlich bist du dir noch großartig vorgekommen, weil du ihr die Freiheit gelassen hast, selbst zu entscheiden . . . Und als sie bei dir blieb, hast du dir auf deine Männlichkeit mächtig was eingebildet" (ibid.). He admits: "Ein Teil des Lebens besteht aus Korrekturen . . ." (ibid.). "Aber das Schuldgefühl meiner Mutter gegenüber trägt er mit sich herum . . ." (ibid.), observes Yana. She asks her mother what her decision would be now if she could choose again. She answers: "Er würde eine solche Forderung nicht mehr stellen . . . . Nein . . . heute nicht mehr" (p. 57). The implication of this remark is that the present time is more progressive, and that her husband has matured in his attitude, which at that time had still been quite bourgeois.

When Yana herself is confronted with the problem of deciding whether she should go to Leningrad to study chemistry, and thus, leave her boy-friend Walter, she faces a somewhat different situation from her mother's. Walter, who is presented as a progressive member of the new society, does not try to influence Yana in his favour; he tells her: "Ich glaube, sie haben recht, und du mußt fahren. Aber ich kann dir nicht zureden, ich bringe es nicht fertig. Mach was" (p. 56). He leaves the decision entirely up to her, and in this case, she obeys her heart, for, as she says: "Ich erkannte, wie sehr er mich liebte, und es machte mich sehr froh. Ich wollte bei ihm bleiben" (ibid.). Walter is understanding, and Yana's decision is a personal and individual one, rather than one which is forced upon her because of the selfish demands of her friend.

Yana's somewhat selfish choice, which is not in accordance with the socialist ideal, perhaps points to her undecidedness and immaturity that lead to her later love affair with Tolja, the outsider, who for a while captures her imagination. The author's main purpose in presenting this incident is to contrast the attitudes of two men, one who is selfish and backward in his views, and one who does not want to put an obstacle in the way of his girl-friend's studies and her duty to society. Walter, who makes speeches and serves on committees, is portrayed as a leader at the university, who is actively engaged in furthering the cause of socialism. Because of his socialist consciousness, he has a more advanced attitude to women.

In Erik Neutsch's *Erzählung* "Akte Nora S.," the heroine is caught in a dilemma, because her lover is not a progressive member of the new society and persists in his bourgeois attitude. The effect of this is reinforced by the fact that her second lover shows a similar attitude towards her. They both see her as someone they need, but do not ask how they can help her in her difficulties with her career, which is important to her and for which she is eminently qualified. They insist on seeing her from the point of view of their own interests and feelings, rather than in terms of what might be best for her, or what might further the development of her talents and personality. Nora becomes "nur das Anhängsel eines Mannes . . ." (p. 237) as she calls it.

The phrase "Ich brauche dich" recurs in the *Erzählung;* it is spoken at different times by the two men in Nora's life, and it expresses for her their egotism and their unwillingness to regard her, not only as a woman they love, but also as an independent designer of machines with an obligation and desire to use her talent in contributing to society. Färber, both her fiancé and her superior at her place of work, grudgingly permits her to go for one week to inspect the pumps she designs: " 'Das ist das höchste,' hatte Färber beim Abschied gesagt, 'doch sieh zu, daß du früher zurückkommst. Ich brauche dich' " (p. 209). But she had hoped for the words: "Ich begreife dich, Nora. Mach deine Sache gut" (p. 237), in the face of her courageous venture.

Later Likendeel uses the same words: "Ich liebe dich. Und ich brauche dich" (p. 242). However, Nora had hoped for his understanding and support:

> Sie sah ihn an und erschrak. Hatte sie das nicht schon einmal, Wort für Wort, von Färber gehört? War es nicht alles dasselbe? . . . Nur nicht schwach werden, dachte sie, nur nicht die eigene Schwäche verraten. . . . Sie wartete auf ein einziges Wort. Ich begreife dich, Nora. Fahr zurück. Bring denen dort bei, was deine Erfindung wert ist . . . So oder ähnlich müßte er sprechen. (ibid.)

Thus, both Likendeel and Färber are caught up in their own selfish attitude towards Nora.

Though she is gifted and clever, and willing to take hardship upon herself for the sake of her work, Erik Neutsch does not present her as a self-sufficient individual. She needs the encouragement and help of men to be able to complete her task. However, it is exactly this that she is not given, because both of these men, who are her superiors at her place of work, fail to take her work seriously. In the end, she finds that arrangements have been made about her future without even consulting her: "Niemand hatte sie nach ihren Wünschen und Plänen gefragt. Die einen so wenig wie die anderen. Sie fühlte sich verkauft" (pp. 241–42). She exclaims bitterly: "Ihr habt mich wie einen Gegenstand, wie ein lebloses Ding verschachert . . ." (p. 242).

Nora is unable to solve the conflict between her career and her love, first for Färber, whom she loses because he does not get his own way, and later, Likendeel, because he does not understand her devotion to her ambitious task and because she does not put him first. "Ich verstehe dich nicht. Wir beide könnten so glücklich sein . . ." (p. 243), Likendeel tells her. Färber observes caustically: "Du fühlst dich nur wohl in deiner Emanzipiertenrolle, und das ist alles. Ich aber, ich liebe die Blaustrümpfe nicht" (p. 236). In contrast to the other men with whom Nora works, only Färber and Likendeel are backward in their attitude towards her, even though they are the ones who love her. Likendeel, for example, shows his conventional bourgeois views, when he exclaims to Nora at her arrival: "Wer hat sich das wieder ausgedacht? Ihr Betrieb scheint nur noch aus Konstruktionsfehlern zu bestehen. Eine Frau . . . Die schickt man doch nicht in den Urwald" (p. 210). The other workers at the geological testing site are at first taken aback at the unaccustomed sight of having a woman in the midst of their hitherto strictly male world. However, as they see her dedication and hard work, their scepticism turns to admiration. When she successfully traces the cause of the defect in the pumps, their recognition of her achievement and their acceptance of her is complete: "Und auch der Meister jubelte, riß sie an sich und stampfte mit ihr in wilden Sprüngen über das Geröll des Bohrfeldes" (p. 240).

Nora is caught in a dilemma. She has a burning desire to complete the task which she feels called to do, but the men who are her superiors at work, whose help and support she needs, do not take her efforts seriously, thinking only of their own interests and desires. Not only her name, but also her situation, caught between the need to be true to herself and the selfishness and backwardness of her lovers, suggest a link with Ibsen's Nora in *A Doll's House*. Erik Neutsch does not directly present a solution in the *Erzählung;* except for his obvious sympathy for the heroine and his depiction of the men's bourgeois attitude, the end is left open. Perhaps, like the heroine of Ibsen's play, Nora has to leave them and find her own way. In her socialist society, she is more advanced and a harmonious solution is not possible unless the men change.

The woman as an individual in her own right

In some *Erzählungen,* the authors are concerned not so much with the woman's career, as with her rights as an individual. They portray women whose relationship with the men they love stifles them rather than helps them to develop their true potential and socialist ideals in their lives.

In Werner Bräunig's *Erzählung* "Unterwegs,"[2] the heroine Sabine Bach leaves her lover David Kroll in anger, when she becomes fully aware of his true attitude towards her. He is selfish and possessive, a man who does not ask about the interests or views of the girl he loves. Regarding Sabine solely from his own point of view, he treats her merely as a beloved object, rather than a person in her own right:

> . . . er hüllte sie in Samt und Seide . . . Ich liebe dich. Ich brauche dich. Und nur eins hat er leider nie gefragt, nämlich was sie denn braucht, was sie denn erwartet von diesem Leben, wohin sie denn will mit sich in unserer Welt. Unmerklich, aber unaufhaltsam sah sie dies: Er forderte sie nicht, er nahm sie. Er richtete ihr Leben ein, er behütete sie, sie stand daneben mit hängenden Armen. . . . Er überhäufte sie mit Aufmerksamkeiten, Zärtlichkeiten, er wollte sie ganz für sich und verlor sie. (p. 151)

As they are driving along on their holiday trip, she insists on being let off on the highway.

---

[2] In *Gewöhnliche Leute.*

When Sabine, emancipated and questioning, met him, he appeared to have the qualities she expected in a man who was a progressive member of the new society:

> Und beinahe folgerichtig hatte sie an dieser Hochschule also einen kennengelernt, der endlich aus einem Guß zu sein schien. Der nahm nichts zurück. Der hielt, was er versprach. Der gab zu, was er nicht wußte, und das als Oberassistent. Der fing nicht zu stottern an angesichts heikler Fragen. Der setzte durch, was als durchsetzenswert erkannt war. (p. 150)

At first she is favourably impressed; however, in his relationship with her, a woman, bourgeois attitudes become apparent and he treats her in a possessive manner. In connection with his possessive attitude, the author suggests, that David Kroll is spoiled and that his socialist values have been corrupted to some extent by his family background, for he emphasizes the point that his father is a "Nationalpreisträger und Städtebauer" (p. 151), and that David has a key to "seines Vaters, des Nationalpreisträgers, erstaunlichem Sommerhaus" (ibid.). Werner Bräunig's character resembles Gerhard Koblenz, the spoiled son of the chief architect in Erik Neutsch's *Erzählung* "Drei Tage unseres Lebens," who also treats women in a very selfish manner. When David Kroll tells Sabine, at the cottage "hätten [wir] endlich mal richtig Zeit für uns . . . wären [wir] endlich allein . . . hätten [wir] Ruhe und überhaupt alles, was wir brauchen" (p. 152), her patience is at an end and she asks him to stop the car. Her sense of values, conditioned by socialist ideals, are incompatible with his attitude.

Werner Bräunig's heroine Sabine Bach is a progressive socialist individual. Though her lover treats her in a selfish and possessive manner, she knows what she wants and is able to assert her rights as a person. Barbara, on the other hand, the protagonist of the story "Einen Californier für meine Frau bitte!"[3] by Lonny Neumann, is not able to assert herself quite as strongly in her relationship with her husband. He makes his decisions without discussing them with his wife, even though they involve her directly, as, for example, his decision to accept a position in another city. He informs her only when the contract has already been signed. Ironically, he is quite unaware of what he is doing to his wife; he discloses the news of his decision to her, for example, as the highlight of a special evening out together in a night club: "Das schlimmste aber war, daß ihr keine andere Wahl blieb. Wolfgang hatte entschieden. Und es hatte sich herausgestellt, daß er nichts, aber auch nichts von ihr wußte" (p. 152). Barbara loves her husband and children, nevertheless, she finds herself, like Nora in "Akte Nora S.," in the position of being "nur das Anhängsel eines Mannes" (Neutsch, p. 237), for, as the author Lonny Neumann observes: "Unmerklich fast war ihr Leben in seine Hände geglitten" (p. 146).

---

[3] In *Zeitzeichen* (Berlin: Buchverlag Der Morgen, [19]68).

Barbara does not know how to change her situation: "Und sie saß nun in dieser Bahn, Station um Station glitt an ihr vorüber, und sie suchte einen Weg, sie selbst zu bleiben" (p. 145).

The thoughtless attitude of her husband stifles her development as a person in her own right. However, the author suggests that her work as a librarian will help her in her struggle. Thus, the story unexpectedly ends on an optimistic note. As Barbara's mind turns to the prospect of the day's work at the library, her courage suddenly returns: "Sie nahm die Umwelt endlich wieder mit der üblichen Schärfe wahr, sah die Sonne, die wohl doch noch Wärme spenden würde, und wußte, daß alles in ihrer Hand lag. Und auch, daß sie Kraft genug für alles besaß" (p. 152). The thought of her work gives her the strength to accept her situation.

Similarly, Brigitte, in Manfred Weinert's *Erzählung* "Strafversetzt"[4] finds a way out of her predicament as a trapped housewife by going back to work after twelve years, because "zu Hause war der Mann wie aus Gußeisen. Neben ihm fühlte sie sich klein in all ihrer Unsicherheit . . ." (p. 67). She is successful in her work and finds herself through it: "Sie war plötzlich wichtig, denn sie hatte Aufträge, und immer wieder: Das hast du gut gemacht, wir haben Vertrauen zu dir. Er aber spürte nicht ihr wachsendes Selbstvertrauen und lachte" (pp. 73–74). The husband stays behind in his development, while she grows: "Ihre Freuden, an denen er nicht teilhatte, waren es, die ihn jetzt blendeten und alles Unfertige in ihm auszuleuchten schienen" (p. 80). As a result of the unexpected emancipation and socialist development of his wife, who has freed herself from the narrow confines of her home, their marriage suffers, because he is not ready to change. The man finds himself imprisoned in a prison of his own making: "Er steht dann im Zimmer, Insel in der Wohnung, er selbst hat es dazu gemacht, ist stolz darauf gewesen, und jetzt steht er da wie eingesperrt" (p. 91).

Thus, the husband, because of his conservative and selfish attitudes, finds himself isolated; his wife, on the other hand, who joins a collective, is able to develop her talents and find herself as a person in her own right. However, the author suggests that the brigade and the amateur performing group at his new place of work will help him and his wife to solve their problems and that it will not come to a divorce after all.

This *Erzählung* is found in an anthology[5] of short prose written largely by amateur writers. In spite of the sometimes exaggerated pathos and simplified characterization, the story throws an interesting sidelight on the relationship of the individual in socialist society, especially in regard to marriage and the working woman. The woman finds her self-realization and meaning in life by working outside of the house; marriage stifles and isolates her. The man must

[4] In *Die vierte Laterne* (Halle/Saale: Mitteldeutscher Verlag, 1971).
[5] *Die vierte Laterne.*

overcome his conservative and selfish attitude in this matter and encourage his wife in her career and share in the housework. If he neglects to do it, he is isolated and left behind in the development of the new society, which is one in which the individual is shaped by his work and his fellow workers, that is, his collective.

Another story in the same anthology, called "Im Kreislauf der Windeln," by Renate Koetter-Johnschker, carries these views even further. Here the domestic role, of staying at home to look after the household and a baby, are negated. It is looked upon as a kind of imprisonment which destroys her personality. The marriage cannot work, implies the author, if the woman does not have an interesting job outside her home.

The woman confronted by a choice

Women are often presented in the *Erzählungen* and *Kurzgeschichten* of the GDR as taking the lead in unselfish action, in making personal choices according to socialist ideals, in moving away from a world of private happiness to an active role in the working world. Women choose the more difficult road of independence, working unselfishly for the good of their society, rather than allowing themselves to be taken care of by a husband or lover, who promises them a private paradise. This is the case in the life of Ute Jager in "Die Versuchung der Ute Jager"[6] by Horst Blume. The story portrays a woman of mature years, who has to choose between a former lover, whom she had thought to be dead, and her village of which she has become the mayor, her life there as part of a collective, and a man she might marry there. The lover tells her:

> Weißt du . . . alles ist hier, alles, was uns Freude schafft. Wir schließen ab und sind in unserer Welt. Du wirst sie uns hüten, Ute, die Verse, Töne und Farben. Es wird nichts geben außer uns. Die Welt draußen ist das Fremde, das Ungemäße. (p. 121)

It is tempting; however, looking back at her hard but rewarding life since they had had to part, she observes:

> Es ist auch, daß ich sie gern gemacht habe, die Arbeit in Pagelow . . . Sie haben mir geholfen, die Genossen und hatten Vertrauen zu mir. Mich hat keiner in die Partei gezwungen, sie haben geglaubt, daß ich zu ihnen gehörte, und all die Jahre hindurch habe ich auch bei ihnen sein wollen. (pp. 121–22)

Ute decides against such a selfish life as that suggested by the lover, though it means denying an earlier part of her life; as a member of socialist society, she

---

[6]   In *Im Strom der Zeit* (Halle/Saale: Mitteldeutscher Verlag, 1965).

accepts the hardships and responsibilities of her present position and duties in the village.

The same choice between a selfish world of two and that of devoting herself to her work, though hard and difficult, is faced by Susanne in Volker Braun's *Erzählung Das ungezwungne Leben Kasts.* At first she succumbs to her difficulties, leaves the city where she has to work, and rejoins Kast. However, their idyll together becomes stale. Finally she makes her decision: "Und ich, geh nach W. zurück" (p. 140). "Wir hatten uns entschieden. Wir würden die Härte auf uns nehmen. Ich war froh und traurig, beides zugleich . . ." (ibid.), observes Kast.

Similarly, Elfi, the heroine of Joachim Nowotny's story "Grog von Rum,"[7] chooses the more difficult path in life for the sake of her ideals and because she wants to be independent. She faces the choice of accepting the offer made by Lässig, a fellow student, to become engaged to him so that she would have an excuse for staying in the city, instead of having to go to a village for her first teaching post:

> Man hätte nur ja sagen müssen, dann wäre man im Handumdrehen verlobt gewesen, verlobt mit einem klugen, sehr tüchtigen Mann, der Schwierigkeiten voraussah und ihnen elegant auswich. . . . Aber Elfi hatte dieses Ja nicht gesagt, sie hatte ihre Erfahrungen selbst gesammelt, es waren bessere, brauchbarere, wenn auch keine bequemen. (p. 42)

Looking back ten years later, she knows she has made the right choice, even though she had a hard time at first: "Die gewöhnlichen Schwierigkeiten des Alltags, die auch in einer Schule mit guter Atmosphäre auftreten, sie reichten völlig hin. Sie wuchsen Elfi bald über den Kopf, den Magen, die Nerven . . ." (p. 41). She observes that she was able to cope, however, "weil man seine Erfahrungen nicht allein machte. Weil man Hilfe fand bei dem Manne, den Kollegen und den Kindern. . . . Das Beste freilich an allem war die Erfahrung, daß man Erfahrung sammeln konnte, daß man nicht so bleiben mußte, wie man war" (pp. 41–42). Thus, her involvement in her work and the collective and her willingness to learn and change, support her in her choice, and help her to find a solution to her problems, while the man, on the other hand, who had offered her an easy way out, is portrayed as one who is selfish and unwilling to become involved in the new society.

In the *Erzählung* "Bitterer Tee"[8] by Ursula Hörig, men are not a factor in the choice a woman has to make, as is usually the case, but the heroine makes a decision to take a certain course, because the life style which another woman represents is unacceptable to her. Gisela Bach, married, with a family, is

---

[7] In *Sonntag unter Leuten* (Halle/Saale: Mitteldeutscher Verlag, 1971).
[8] In *Die vierte Laterne.*

studying for an engineering degree by correspondence. Feeling unusually weary and discouraged, she visits a childhood friend. When she sees her preoccupation with holiday trips, cosmetics, her house, and playing cards, Gisela decides that her own path, though difficult, is the better one: "Sie hatte also an der verkehrten Stelle ein Gespräch gesucht. Vertane Zeit? . . . War da nicht die Erkenntnis, so wie Susanne nicht leben zu können . . . Sie würde immer ein Ziel brauchen, immer die Unruhe, nicht genug zu wissen" (p. 150).

All of these *Erzählungen* present vital choices which the women make. The kind of choice they make reveals their relationship to the new society; it is like a test which shows whether they are living according to its values.

Die bewußte Frau

The emancipated woman is best characterized by the word *bewußt* or *selbst-bewußt,* an adjective frequently used to describe a heroine in a literary work of the GDR. Even where the word is not used directly, the quality it represents is implied in her actions or attitude. Adele Noth, the heroine of Werner Bräunig's *Erzählung* "Gewöhnliche Leute," who is an example of an individual in socialist society, possesses this quality: "Sie war also ins Gelände gekommen mit der spöttischen Selbstverständlichkeit dieser Sorte Mädchen, die bloß noch auffällt, wenn man darüber nachdenkt . . ." (p. 14). She is poised and at ease, sure of herself and knows that she has her own important contribution to make.

In the same way, Rita in Benito Wogatzki's *Erzählung* "Der Preis des Mädchens" shows by her actions and attitude that she is *selbst-bewußt.* She knows what she wants and is able to plot her own course. When she discovers that her lover has left her, she decides not to tell him that she is expecting his child:

> Diesen Trumpf in der Hand, hatte sie sich dann selbst auf den Weg gemacht. Sie hatte ein Kind bekommen, aber sie hatte nicht ihre Freiheit, ihren Schwung eingebüßt, sie war von da an wieder zur Schule gegangen. (p. 24)

She says to Möllenthin: "Ich hatte plötzlich keine Zeit mehr. Hab mir gedacht, gehst am besten schon immer alleine los" (p. 25). Thus she is "arbeiten gegangen wie ein Maurer, hat die Mutter gepflegt, ist zur Schule gelaufen jeden Abend wie andere zum Dienst . . ." (p. 24). Möllenthin observes admiringly: "Das ist so, wie wenn Blumen übers Wetter lachen . . . Wetterfeste Blumen sozusagen, die der Frost nicht erreichen kann. Die kann anfassen was sie will, sie macht sich nicht schmutzig dabei. Die lebt viel zu sehr" (ibid.). In this way, the author, Benito Wogatzki, portrays a model of the *bewußte Frau.*

Another such heroine is Sabine Bach in "Unterwegs" by Werner Bräunig. She, too, is equal to her situation; when the truck driver who gives her a ride has a flat tire, she helps him like an expert, with poise and self-confidence:

> Und sie hatte nun den obligaten Ölfleck im Gesicht und half das alte Rad herunterheben und das neue hinauf. Das ging ihr alles von der Hand. Natürlich fragte Karl, ob sie dergleichen schon einmal gemacht habe, an einem PKW vielleicht. Sie lächelte und sagte: 'Nicht daß ich wüßte.' (p. 144)

She displays the kind of self-confidence which characterizes the woman of the new society who is *bewußt*.

It is striking how capable these women are. In Helmut Sakowski's story "Wie sich das Nachdenken ausgezahlt hat," Elli-Marie, "eine attraktive junge Dame . . . energischen Schrittes . . . selbstbewußt, wortgewandt und fest entschlossen . . ." (p. 205), has studied agricultural science, is married with two children, and directs the co-operative academy of an LPG: "Und die schweren Männer, obwohl sie mit dem Mädchen manches Wortgefecht zu bestehen haben, sind stolz auf die schöne Elli-Marie, die Chefin ihrer Kooperationsakademie . . ." (p. 204).

Die bewußte Frau, as portrayed in *Erzählungen* of the GDR, is emancipated from the traditional role of women, and in her new role she reveals the changes peculiar to the society of the GDR. This exemplary woman incorporates in her attitude to life and in her view of the world the ideals of socialism. Above all else, she has a socialist personality. Werner Jehser states:

> Die Gesellschaft existiert nach marxistisch-leninistischer Auffassung nicht nur außerhalb der Persönlichkeit, sondern gewissermaßen auch in ihr, in ihrer Lebenseinstellung und ihrer Weltanschauung, in ihren Empfindungen und Gefühlen, in ihren ethischen Grundsätzen.[9]

However, there are a few minor negative female characters. Hertha, the wife of the innkeeper Schorsch in Werner Bräunig's *Erzählung* "Der Hafen der Hände,"[10] lives a loose moral life and does not possess a socialist consciousness. She needs help and guidance, if she is to become an integrated individual of socialist society. She is, however, only mentioned in the story and serves as a contrast to the positive female characters Paula, the capable "Fachmethodikerin beim Bezirksrat" and Anne Müller, the "Zootechnikerin," women who are *bewußt* and who play an active role in society. In the story "Bitterer Tee" by Ursula Hörig, the selfish and self-indulgent Susanne stands out in marked contrast to the protagonist Gisela Bach.

---

[9] "Zum neuen Charakter des literarischen Konflikts," *WB,* 16, No. 2 (1970), p. 102.
[10] In *Gewöhnliche Leute.*

Ursula, the wayward wife of Ham, the truck driver, in Benito Wogatzki's "Ein Tag und eine Nacht" also represents a woman who lacks a socialist consciousness, because in her youth she did not have the opportunity of learning to become a better citizen. Except for Susanne, who is simply presented as a contrast to the protagonist, Hertha and Ursula are portrayed as women who have not been given a chance and who took the wrong turn in their lives due to lack of guidance. These characters help to show that women must recognize the need for acquiring a consciousness of their role in society and cannot just play it instinctively; they have to be made aware of their new role.

Harmonious partnerships

Whenever a harmonious relationship between men and women is portrayed, both individuals are well integrated in the new society and both possess a socialist consciousness. This type of ideal relationship is found mainly in Werner Bräunig's *Erzählungen*. There is no friction; both characters are progressive and are fully adjusted to socialist society. The shining examples are Adele Noth and Hannes Stütz, their friends Eva Moßmann and her husband, in "Gewöhnliche Leute," Hanna and Peter Trumm in "Der schöne Monat August," Stefan and his future wife in "Die einfachste Sache der Welt," and Anne and Jakob Müller in "Der Hafen der Hände." Also, Kast and Susanne in Volker Braun's *Erzählung Das ungezwungne Leben Kasts,* and Regine and Richard in Fritz Rudolf Fries' *Erzählung* "Beschreibung meiner Freunde,"[11] exemplify such a relationship.

In all cases both the men and the women have a profession or a trade; the women are equal in their education with that of the men. They are successful in their work and they respect each other's contribution. Stefan in Bräunig's "Die einfachste Sache der Welt" admires the accomplishments of his girl-friend:

> Und wahrscheinlich, dachte er, würde auch keiner, der sie jetzt sah, darauf kommen, daß sie als Landmaschinenschlosser arbeitet und mit allerhand handfesten Sachen umgehen kann. Etwas anderes waren da schon die Kupferarbeiten, die sie anfertigte, auch die Teppiche, die sie knüpfte, und das tat sie also nebenbei. Wahrhaftig, dachte er, das ist schon'ne Menge erstaunlicher Sachen. (p. 74)

It is taken for granted that the women work; for example, when Jakob Müller in Bräunig's "Der Hafen der Hände" is asked if his wife works, too, he replies: "Sicher . . . Zootechnikerin. Sie geht zur Genossenschaft" (p. 85).

---

[11] In *Prosa aus der DDR* (Paderborn: Schöningh, 1969).

In Fritz Rudolf Fries' *Erzählung* "Beschreibung meiner Freunde," Richard
and Regine are both medical doctors; theirs is a harmonious partnership of give
and take:

> Hier unter der Lampe, am Abend, glaubt sie, ein einmaliges schönes glückliches Leben
> zu haben. ... für ihr eigenes Glücklichsein, glaube ich, verteilt sie am Tage die
> Medikamente, gibt Injektionen, tut ihr Äußerstes, telefoniert in den Pausen mit
> Richard, um seine Stimme aus dem anderen Ende der Stadt zu hören und ihn zu
> bitten, Sabine vom Kindergarten abzuholen, die Milch im Konsum nicht zu vergessen
> und das Weißbrot: sie kommt doch später als angenommen. (p. 128)

Their busy life is anchored in a stable relationship. This is also the case with
Hanna and Peter Trumm in "Der schöne Monat August", and, in fact, with all
the other couples mentioned above. Trumm remarks good-humouredly: "Bei
anderen wackeln die Wände, bei uns wackeln sie nicht, das ist ja ganz schön. . . .
Diese Geschichte mit der stets gleichbleibenden Durchschnittstemperatur"
(p. 103). Adele Noth and Hannes Stütz in "Gewöhnliche Leute" are presented
as complementing each other in their work and their personalities, as an ideal
couple. Stütz shows understanding and sympathy for Adele's work and
problems, but lets her do what she has to do on her own:

> Stütz hatte sich die Proben aus dem Institut angesehen, das Projekt leuchtete ihm ein
> ... Aber er hielt sich heraus. Er wußte, daß sie da durch mußte. Es war ihre erste
> große Arbeit, und sie durfte nicht das Gefühl haben, geschoben zu werden – schon gar
> nicht von ihm. (p. 31)

Thus, co-operation and mutual respect mark their relationship, especially in the
area of their work.

According to the *Erzählungen,* these personal relationships are possible,
because of the stable foundation offered by socialist society to those who are
integrated members of it. However, where the women are more progressive or
are held back by the bourgeois attitude of the men, which are the situations
presented in other *Erzählungen* mentioned in this chapter, this harmony is not
possible. Thus, in Werner Bräunig's "Unterwegs," Sabine Bach has to leave her
lover David Kroll, because of his possessive and selfish attitude; however, the
man who gives her a ride is a true socialist, as Sabine is herself, and their
budding friendship promises to develop into a closer bond. As Sabine helps him
to change a flat tire, their mutual give and take suggests an equal partnership:

> Sie kam aber doch herausgeklettert. Hatte das Kopftuch wieder umgetan, hatte sich
> Karls alte Drillichjacke angezogen und die Ärmel aufgerollt: ein erstaunlicher Anblick.
> Und während Karl das Reserverad vom Wagen holte, setzte sie schon den Wagenheber
> an. An der richtigen Stelle. Karl lockerte die Muttern, sie schraubte sie herunter.
> Nebenbei sagte sie, sie hieße Sabine. Arbeit, heißt es, bringt die Menschen einander
> näher: Das ist wahr. (p. 144)

From the stories it is evident that the stability of a relationship in the new society is based on two foundation stones: work and the collective. Thus, as Sabine and the truck driver work together side by side, their activity serves as a common bond between them. This is also true of Adele Noth and Hannes Stütz in "Gewöhnliche Leute," and of "Die einfachste Sache der Welt," in which the author, Werner Bräunig, implies that the couples harmonize so well, because each person is deeply involved in his or her work and feels secure in it. The author also shows that the individuals do not exist in isolation, but are members of a collective. Whereas in "Unterwegs" David Kroll is presented as the spoiled son of a rich and successful father, and thus stands, as it were, alone in society, the student, turned truck driver, who is the new, and more worthy, friend of Sabine Bach, is a member of a collective. Werner Bräunig uses the term "seine Leute" in speaking of him: "Es war mal einer, den schickten seine Leute zum Studium, und er seinerseits kam in den Sommerferien für drei Wochen in den Betrieb, damit seine Leute auch mal Sommerurlaub hätten" (p. 142). Thus, work and the collective form the basis of a stable relationship between the sexes, provided that the individuals involved are both progressive and well integrated members of their society.

Marriage and the new role of women

Marriage becomes a topic of discussion in some *Erzählungen* in the light of the new role of women in socialist society. In Werner Bräunig's "Der schöne Monat August," Peter Trumm listens to a lecture on love and marriage:

> Der Nervendoktor hatte ... auf einem Vortrag vom Kulturbund erzählt ... die Liebe sei mehr was fürs Individuum, die Ehe mehr was für die Gesellschaft. ... Also ein Sakrament, hatte er gesagt, ist die Ehe nicht, sondern eine Gesellschaftsfunktion ... (p. 103)

Dr. Niebergall tells his audience that the present form of marriage, based on monogamy, may change; however, he observes: "Was danach kommt, kann ich von meinem Fachgebiet aus nicht mit Sicherheit sagen" (p. 104). Thus, if marriage is seen as a function of society, then, within socialist society, new forms of the relationship between the sexes may emerge, a possibility, however, which only a few authors, chiefly Volker Braun in his *Erzählung Das ungezwungne Leben Kasts,* pursue in their stories. In Braun's work, Hagen and Linde are staunch supporters of marriage, while the hero Kast is in the process of discovering alternative forms for himself. A kind of Faust, "unfähig zu jeglicher Bindung" (p. 60), he decides to leave Linde, who seeks marriage in its traditional sense.

Volker Braun makes the problem of marriage in terms of socialism a prominent theme in his work, and theoretical discussions of it occur at various points in the narrative.[12] The implication is made that in this area the individual must find a new kind of relationship. For Kast work takes precedence over his personal life. He sees love, therefore, as something which is modified by, and related to, the role of work in an individual's life:

> Auch die Liebe ist eine Produktion. Wenn der Forscher drauf brennt, einen lebensgefährlichen Virus zu finden — und was ist Liebe dann andres, die das Bett oder die Wiese zu ihrer Aktion braucht statt dem Mikroskop oder der Retorte? Wenn der Forscher den Virus auffindet, ist seine unbändige Liebe zu dieser Forschung erfüllt und am Ende. Er wird seine Leidenschaft auf einen andern Gegenstand werfen — der erste ist abgetan. (pp. 79–80)

Kast and Susanne decide to separate, so that each will be free to pursue his or her respective work in different towns, and meet whenever they can. Susanne declares, that although she would like to stay with her lover, each one should do what is right for him: " 'Und doch — müßte jeder leben wie er muß,' sagte sie, 'wie es für *ihn* richtig ist!' " (p. 137). The author suggests that their willingness to be unselfish and to allow each other their individual freedom will enrich and deepen their relationship and love for each other.

Kast and Susanne represent the new objective view of love propounded in Volker Braun's *Erzählung.* Linde, whom Kast leaves, is too dependent and emotional, and she insists on marriage; her views are associated with bourgeois sentimentality. Similarly, in Werner Heiduczek's *Erzählung Mark Aurel oder ein Semester Zärtlichkeit,* Tolja is portrayed as being sentimental and emotional, and, at the same time, as being selfish and lacking a socialist consciousness. Even though Yana is swept along by his love for a while, she has to leave him because he does not fit into the new society.

The *Erzählungen,* on the whole, do not offer anything approaching a definition of love or marriage in socialism. In a number of stories, the author suggests that there is a change from the dark past to a bright present in which women are free. Werner Bräunig, in his *Erzählung* "Die einfachste Sache der Welt," has the hero considering what would have happened if the woman he hopes to marry had lived before the advent of socialism:

> Und was wäre vor zwanzig und einigen Jahren aus solcher Mädchenfrau geworden? Darauf hat man Antworten. Rings eine Weltkonferenz unglaublicher Einöden, und im Schweiße deines Angesichts sollst du deinem Brotherrn dienen und nicht begehren den Blick über die Kirchturmspitze . . . (p. 77)

The society of the GDR is one which makes the best life possible for the woman and gives her a new role based on her position as a worker and as a member of a collective. An observation made by Arno Hochmuth sums up the new attitude:

[12] See, for example, pp. 55, 80, 83.

Die Beziehungen zum anderen Geschlecht, zur Familie machen unter sozialistischen Bedingungen eine reale Revolution durch. Sie erreichen erst in dieser Gesellschaft den Charakter wahrer Gleichberechtigung und gegenseitiger kameradschaftlicher Achtung.[13]

---

[13] "Unsere neue Wirklichkeit literarisch erobern: Der VII. Parteitag und unsere Literatur," in *Kritik in der Zeit,* p. 818.

Chapter V

THE OUTSIDER

Helmut Sakowski begins his story "Die Aussteuer" with the words:

> Mal unter uns: Schwer mit der Kunst. Alles schon dagewesen. Da gibt es die Geschichte vom Einzelgänger, den das böse Kollektiv verkennt, und die vom jungen Mann, der zum Rebellen wird, weil das Leben anders ist, als es die Schule lehrte, und die vom verdienten Alten, der heutzutage nicht mehr mitkommt . . .[1]

This passage throws an interesting side light on some of the themes that have been popular in the literature of the GDR. Almost without exception, the individuals mentioned are in some way outsiders of the new society.

An outsider because of old age

Werner Heiduczek, in his *Kurzgeschichte* "Das zwölfte Buch,"[2] portrays an old writer who has outlived his fame and productivity. In his youth, he had been one of the fighters of socialism, and when the new society was being established in the GDR, he was mayor of a town and, at the same time, a writer of books which were in great demand. Now they have outlived their popularity, and he himself is old and cannot keep up with recent developments in his country. He suddenly finds himself alone and outside the society, which he had helped to build. " 'Du deutest, mein Lieber, die Dinge falsch,' " he is told patronizingly by his younger colleagues at the writers' club. "Das hieß, du verstehst sie nicht mehr. Du bist alt geworden. So einfach war das" (p. 360). They tolerate him as a harmless old man, and his exclusion is obvious.

In a socialist society, in which work plays a vital role, the old man's situation is tragic. It is essential for him to be useful and to be a part of society: "Er konnte nicht leben, ohne da mittendrin zu stecken. Er brauchte das alles: den Gemeinderat, den Schulneubau, die Genossenschaft" (pp. 362–63). However, now he is confronted with a new and uncomfortable situation, in which he is helpless: "Was war aus ihm geworden? Was war von seinen Hoffnungen geblieben? Von seiner Kraft? Es war ein ganz neues Gefühl in ihm. Er bekam Angst davor" (p. 363). The pathos of the words, "Ein solches Gefühl der Verlassenheit hatte er nicht einmal während des Krieges in seiner Einzelzelle in Moabit gehabt" (p. 365), especially expresses his loneliness and isolation.

---

[1] In *Zwei Zentner Leichtigkeit,* p. 130.
[2] In *Bettina pflückt wilde Narzissen.*

He cannot give up writing, because this would mean relinquishing his purpose for living. He makes a renewed resolution to keep on writing his twelfth book, though he knows he cannot finish it anymore. Though the story ends with the remark: "Heute nacht wollte er anfangen" (p. 367), there is no suggestion of hope that he will succeed or find a solution to his dilemma. Since an individual is valued according to his productivity and ability to work, the old man, who has outlived this period of his life, becomes an outsider.

A similar theme is found in the *Kurzgeschichte* "Josefski" by Bernd Jentzsch. The protagonist Josefski has spent a long and useful life serving his society, but now, because of old age and lack of training, he is not able to keep up with the most recent advances in the world around him, and, as a result, he finds that he has become an outsider. Sent to a health resort by his collective, he tries to come to grips with his situation and to get well as soon as possible by participating faithfully in all the activities there. However, his life of work and usefulness is over; this is a bitter truth to face for a man to whom it is essential to be able to contribute to society. Josefski thinks: "Ja, notwendig zu sein, ist einer der erregendsten Gedanken" (p. 241). The *Kurzgeschichte* ends with these words and the author offers no solution.

Werner Bräunig offers a temporary solution in his *Erzählung* "Stillegung" by having the protagonist, an old pensioner, find another form of employment, this time as a night watchman. In this way, he can contribute to society again and overcome his isolation. Similarly, in Erwin Strittmatter's *Erzählung* "Kraftstrom," the protagonist, old Adam, finds a useful occupation again by repairing the electric fences on the LPG.

In their *Kurzgeschichten,* Heiduczek and Jentzsch depict the situation in which their protagonists, old and unable to cope, suddenly find themselves. In a society which places the chief value on work and productivity, these men become outsiders. Without directly acknowledging the dilemma of the individual who is old and disabled, the authors do raise the question implicitly. However, no attempt is made to answer it, nor even to justify or criticize this aspect of socialism.

Bräunig and Strittmatter offer a temporary solution to the dilemma by portraying the happiness of the old men as they take up their newly found tasks. However, they evade the actual problem, since there will come a time when they will be unable to keep up with their work.

Among the few stories in the literature of the GDR that mention death, two of them deal with old men who have reached the end of their lives. They are presented as being unusually active and so involved and interested in their work, that they are occupied with it until their last conscious moment. In this way the problem and the loneliness of old age and its accompanying disability are dealt with from the standpoint of the socialist view of life and the concept of the "positive" hero.

In the *Erzählung* "Der letzte Streich" by Benito Wogatzki, Papa Kolbe, a man in his eighties, cannot die because he is too curious and interested in the latest developments at the industrial plant in which he used to work even after his retirement. His doctor observes: "Klinisch ist er schon seit drei Jahren tot, aber er kann vor Neugier nicht sterben" (p. 50). Once, when Papa Kolbe seemed to be dying, Schemmel, his former protégé, had to come and tell him the latest news at the plant: "Schemmel saß vier Stunden an seinem Bett, mußte Schnaps trinken und reden. Einfach so. Immer nur reden. Und Kolbe lag da, die großen Hände auf dem Deckbett, das Gesicht feierlich rasiert und die Ohren sperrangelweit auf" (p. 49). He recovers again and continues his activities: "Bald darauf trat der schon Totgeglaubte mit seinem Milchbeutelskandal wieder ins öffentliche Leben . . ." (p. 69).

His deep interest in his former work and in the progress of the industrial plant, to which he has contributed so much in his life, spur him on. When he finally dies, he does so while listening with all his might to Schemmel telling him about the latest advances in the methods of production and in the research which he is directing at the plant. As the younger man suddenly realizes that Kolbe is dead, he says: "Aber mitbekommen hast du's noch! Natürlich! Ich kenn dich doch!" (p. 80).

The *Erzählung* "Das Testament"[3] by Joachim Nowotny contains a similar theme. On his deathbed, the old brigadier Paul Jork musters his remaining strength to give a list of instructions about what remains to be done on the LPG. He dies as he is in the midst of doing this. Work is so important to this man that he keeps on working up to the moment when he collapses from a stroke, and even at the last moment of his life, all his thoughts revolve around his duties and responsibilities. Thinking over Paul Jork's life, the Chairman of the LPG concludes:

> Wer sich kräftig in sein Joch beugt, der zerbricht es nach und nach. Ist aber einer darunter, dessen Kraft von jahrzehntelanger Plackerei zerstört wurde, so wird er zwar in den Sielen zusammenbrechen aber nie vor seiner Zeit sterben. (p. 255)

Thus, whatever aspect of life the writer of socialist realism deals with, he treats it from the standpoint of the socialist view of the world. The loneliness of the individual in sickness or in death is not mentioned, since this would be at odds with the concept of the "positive" hero. Even in death, for these two old men, their work is their chief value and goal. The authors overcome the problem of old age and disability by not allowing these men to become outsiders, but letting them go on with their tasks until the last moment of their lives.

---

[3] In *Im Strom der Zeit.*

An outsider because of immaturity

A type of outsider presented in a number of stories is an immature young person who does not have a well-developed socialist consciousness and who, for various reasons, has negative feelings towards his society. He is therefore isolated. But as he grows in maturity and insight or, as in several cases, falls in love with a girl who has a socialist awareness, the individual changes. The situation of being an outsider is a temporary one for him, marking but a stage in his development. In the end, he arrives at a meaningful relationship with his collective and the rest of society.

In the *Erzählung* "Podiralla geht zum Zirkus"[4] by Kristian Pech, the young hero finds himself at odds with society and goes off to a lonely spot in the country to think about his situation. The reason for his self-imposed isolation is a personal disappointment caused by an injustice which he has suffered. Podiralla has been refused permission for further study. "Mir wurde Unreife bescheinigt," he states. "Und ich glaube kaum, daß meine Mitschüler reifer waren. Aber sie haben die Unehrlichkeit eines Lehrers geduldet" (p. 207). Hurt and disappointed, he plans to join the circus: "Im September geh' ich zum Zirkus. Ich sollte eigentlich in einem Großbetrieb arbeiten, damit ich in ein starkes Kollektiv hineinwachsen kann, hieß es" (p. 207).

However, in his stay in the country, he falls in love with Wera, who does not approve of his idea of joining the circus. She remarks: "Man hat dir unrecht getan, nehmen wir an. Man hat einen Fehler gemacht. Du aber machst tausend, wenn du so über die Welt philosophierst. Das geht nicht" (p. 210). Podiralla's growing love for Wera gives him a new sense of purpose and direction. This process is underscored by an incident which Wera tells him:

> In das Haus, in dem ich wohne, zog vor zwei Jahren ein Ehepaar . . . Die beiden lernten sich über den Zaun der Strafanstalt hinweg kennen. . . . Die Frau, wegen Arbeits-bummelei verurteilt, war seit der Stunde der Bekanntschaft wie umgewandelt. Die Strafvollzieher merkten das . . . Sie wurde frühzeitig entlassen. Ehe sie ins Dorf kamen, heirateten die beiden. Und jetzt ist die Frau Brigadier. (p. 210)

In the same way, Podiralla is transformed by his love, and he makes a decision: "Ich geh nicht zum Zirkus. Ich bleib' in diesem Nest" (p. 212). His disappointment and his feeling that an injustice has been done to him quickly melt, as he falls in love. He thus joins the new society.

In Erwin Strittmatter's *Erzählung* "Bedenkzeit," Eddie Kienast loses his position as the chairman of an LPG, because of his backward attitude. As a result of his demotion, he sulks and assumes the role of an outsider. "Von diesem Augenblick an lief die Versammlung ohne mich weiter. Ich saß in einem

---

[4] In *Bettina pflückt wilde Narzissen.*

Ruderboot, hatte mein Ruder eingezogen . . ." (p. 242), he observes. He lacks a fully developed socialist consciousness, and consequently, his relationship with others deteriorates, even that with his own family. He becomes estranged from his wife, who is active in all the affairs of the LPG: "Wir lebten wie zwei Länder, die die diplomatischen Beziehungen zueinander nicht abbrechen, weil sie noch einige gemeinsame Interessen haben . . ." (p. 250).

However, after gaining insight into his responsibility to others, and learning about the possibilities open to him and to the other members of the LPG in regard to technological progress, he is able to come to terms with himself. He accepts what had seemed to him a humiliation, and even overcomes his antipathy for his rival Glante, the chairman of the LPG. Kienast shares his newly discovered technical information about the building of an ultra-modern pig barn with him. Furthermore, he decides to support the collective wholeheartedly, showing by his actions his change of heart and growth in maturity. Thus, "der ehemalige Vorsitzende, Genosse Kienast, der lange abseits stand" (p. 245), becomes at the end an example of a progressive individual of the society of the GDR: "Sein Gesicht glänzte. In diesem Augenblick schien er mir Glante überlegen zu sein, der vielleicht mit dem Bau des großen Stalles am Ziel seiner Wünsche angelangt war" (p. 263). Kienast now wants to forge ahead and to improve his training and his ability to contribute to his collective.

The same theme appears in the first part of Volker Braun's *Erzählung Das ungezwungne Leben Kasts,* as the author shows how his protagonist becomes a member of a socialist society. At the beginning of the narrative, Kast goes through a negative phase marked by isolation. A disappointed young man who is an outsider, he is critically disposed towards the new society, and he is expelled from school for voicing his criticisms. The author suggests that he is immature, and that he has not yet experienced the feeling of being part of a collective, of working side by side with others at a common task. The fact that he is an outsider and not a participator in the life of his society is expressed by the image of the river. At first he looks at it passively from the shore: "Ich saß lange, ich war froh, stundenlang so zu sitzen, nichts tun, nur hinabsehn! Weiter wollte ich nichts . . ." (p. 15). In a dramatic moment, when the brigade toils all night in an emergency situation, he becomes a participator and becomes one with the others. He declares: "Ich hatte noch nie eine solche Beziehung zu den Dingen um mich gehabt . . . jetzt floß eine große vollgefüllte Landschaft um mich . . . Dieses seltsame Gefühl — wie in einem Fluß zu stehn . . ." (p. 33). A lonely, disappointed, and immature outsider becomes a member of society.

Manfred Jendryschik also takes up the popular theme of the young and immature outsider in his *Kurzgeschichte* "Briefe."[5] A series of short letters written by a girl to a boy-friend reveal her immaturity and, in contrast, his well-developed socialist consciousness. Her own lack of it is shown especially

[5] In *Glas und Ahorn.*

clearly by her predilection for popular songs on West German radio stations, which in East Germany are associated with decadence and the propagation of bourgeois values. She is temporarily expelled from school: "Weil ich das schon immer treibe (Schlager hören), hat das Pädagogische Institut beschlossen, ich soll mein Studium für ein Jahr unterbrechen. Um die richtige Reife zu bekommen" (p. 78). She moves from place to place with no fixed commitments. Finally, after many mistakes, she attains a measure of insight into herself as she accepts her pregnancy and her circumstances: "Ich glaube, ich habe eine Masse Quatsch hinter mir," she admits, "vielleicht muß man noch mal anfangen . . ." (p. 84).

In the stories discussed above, the outsiders, most of them young and immature, need to undergo a process of education and to gain new insight into themselves and their relationship to their society, before they can become members of it. This process consists mainly in their learning to set aside private feelings and selfish demands and to commit themselves to the common goal of the society of the GDR. It may well be assumed that the situation of these outsiders is typical of many young people in the GDR and that these stories aim at educating them.

The outsider portrayed as a negative example

In some *Erzählungen*, the figure of an outsider who is completely negative is portrayed to serve as a contrast to the "positive" hero. Two such examples are Gerhard Koblenz in Erik Neutsch's *Erzählung* "Drei Tage unseres Lebens," and Scherbath in Manfred Jendryschik's *Kurzgeschichte* "Der Alte und die Möwen."[6] Whereas in the narratives mentioned in the preceding section, the immaturity of the protagonist is responsible for his isolation, which is overcome as he grows in maturity and gains insight, these two characters do not change or find a way of joining the new society.

In Erik Neutsch's *Erzählung*, "Drei Tage unseres Lebens," Gerhard Koblenz, "das Söhnchen von einem Arzt oder einem Direktor oder was sonst aus einer verwöhnten Familie . . ." (p. 191), stands out as a negative contrast to the main characters, Konz and Brüdering, and, in fact, to all the other characters. He is intelligent and a leader in his class in school, but also a disrupting influence. Brüdering observes: "Ein Dickschädel wie sein Vater. . . . Auch er war der Wortführer seiner Klasse. Intelligent wie Einstein. Auch auf ihn schworen die Mitschüler. Außer in Mathematik, Physik und Chemie störte er jeden Unterricht" (p. 170). He cheats in school and is morally corrupt. He is the cause of Sigrid Seidensticker's running away from home. Brüdering says of

6   In *Glas und Ahorn*.

him that in his relationship to the opposite sex, he is "älter als ein alter Mann" (p. 192). As in Manfred Jendryschik's "Briefe," Gerhard's utter lack of socialist values is represented by his listening to jazz and popular modern music on the West German radio. Furthermore, his den in the basement, decorated with gaudy and risqué posters, suggesting a hippie environment, points to his decadence. Konz, the Party secretary and "positive" hero of the *Erzählung,* feels contempt for him: "Sie sind zu bedauern. Sie sind so primitiv und dumm wie . . . das Gedudel vom Deutschlandfunk" (pp. 191–92). Brüdering feels that Gerhard Koblenz' father has been much too lenient, calling his son "Einstein" and excusing his behaviour because of his intelligence. The author does not bring out any redeeming features in him at all. He thus stands out, in contrast to the other figures in the story, as an outsider.

Another character who is an outsider because he is a poor socialist, is the old man in Manfred Jendryschik's *Kurzgeschichte* "Der Alte und die Möwen." The figure of Scherbath is pathetic and tragic. Keule, a young man, finds him unexpectedly, isolated and unemployed, living alone in a ramshackle cabin by the sea shore. He has once owned an iron factory and now he makes no effort to contribute to the new society. Scherbath is contrasted in Keule's mind with one of his fellow workers, Sergius, also an older man,

> der Alte mit den Riesenohren, dessen Finger nicht ausreichten, um seine Berufe aufzuzählen, als letzten Revolverdreher, und das hatte ihn in die Zeitung gebracht, da standen sie alle: Tagelöhner am Bau, Landarbeiter, Häuer, Häftling, Soldat, Hilfsarbeiter, Abgeordneter, Bürgermeister, Bäcker, Dreher, Brigadier. Und dreimal Aktivist . . . seine Norm schafften die Jungen kaum . . . (pp. 171–72)

In contrast, Scherbath's lack of a socialist consciousness is shown by his aimless and meaningless existence, suggested, for example, by his repetitive and useless feeding of the seagulls on the beach. The young man sees no hope for change in him; when he sees him feeding the gulls again, he knows that he will keep on doing this; it is "ein ewiger Alptraum" (p. 173). He is a negative character, who helps Keule to learn a lesson about socialist society, as he contrasts in his mind the worker-hero Sergius and the outsider Scherbath. He knows to which world he belongs, as he leaves the lonely beach and hurries back to town, where the others live and work. The beach and the town offer in this *Kurzgeschichte* a further contrast between the figure of the outsider and the community with which Keule identifies himself even more consciously after his encounter with Scherbath.

The outsider and the collective

The *Erzählung Er kam mit dem Herbstwind*[7] by Martin Selber deals with the theme of the relationship of the outsider and the collective. Bernhard, the central character, has been an outsider or *Einzelgänger,* as he is referred to in the narrative, all his life. He is restless and rootless, changes jobs often, and does not want to commit himself to a collective. His excellent work, which often causes envy, accompanied by his lack of committed effort in trying to cope with problems that may arise as people work together, soon leads to friction. Whenever a situation becomes uncomfortable for him, he leaves. This pattern repeats itself every time he comes to a new town to work in its LPG. Karin, a former love of his, whom he meets again by chance many years later on the LPG which is the setting of this story, comments that he is

> nur für sich da . . . für sein eigenes verkorkstes Leben. Er will sich nicht festlegen, nicht binden, um keinen Preis. Jetzt begreife ich erst, warum die Brigade ihn nicht mag, warum er nirgends warm wird unter den Menschen. Er will seine Eitelkeit nähren. (p. 117)

The author shows here that an individual is an outsider because of egoism and vanity, giving priority to his private feelings and seeking honour for himself. Another facet of the outsider Bernhard is suggested by the young worker Heiner, who observes: "Er kennt kein Vertrauen, nie und nirgendwo, und darum bleibt er draußen auf der Landstraße" (p. 105). He is not able, or does not desire, to commit himself to the collective.

However, society and the collective, which represent the right way, win in his life. The *Erzählung* shows that the collective has the strength within itself to be able to educate and to integrate the individual who is outside of it. Various people in the village help Bernhard to overcome the difficulties which arise. Ina wins his love and commitment; the others show understanding. Reuter, his superior at the LPG, expresses a positive attitude towards the perennial outsider: "Die Unruhvollen wecken unsre Aktivität, man muß sie halten, ins Kollektiv zwingen, nicht weiter schicken" (p. 169). In the end, he decides to stay permanently.

The outsider as an exotic element

In some *Erzählungen,* the figure of the outsider is associated with an exotic element, which attracts and fascinates the staid and well-integrated members of the society. In Martin Selber's *Er kam mit dem Herbstwind,* one of the

---

[7]   In *Er kam mit dem Herbstwind* (Halle/Saale: Mitteldeutscher Verlag, 1970).

characters, Karin, says of Bernhard, the rootless wanderer and outsider: "Wir haben uns doch eingerichtet und unsern Platz gefunden, und wir blechen. – Bloß manchmal, da will man weg für eine Weile, andere Bilder sehen, andere Menschen" (p. 175). She is a hardworking and faithful member of the collective of her village, but Bernhard awakens within her a longing for something new and different. However, this is only a passing theme in the story; Bernhard is the one who changes and eventually settles down to share their kind of life.

This theme of the momentary fascination of the exotic or unusual also appears in Werner Heiduczek's *Erzählung Mark Aurel oder ein Semester Zärtlichkeit.* Yana is attracted to the protagonist Tolja, an outsider. She remarks: "Es mag eine alberne Romantik von mir sein, aber ich habe immer Sehnsucht nach etwas Verrücktem. Vielleicht, weil ich so langweilig normal bin" (p. 24). A member of the new society, Yana is, nevertheless, drawn away for a while by her attraction for this young man and what he represents to her. In an interview, the author observed about his character Tolja: "Er reißt für Yana eine neue Ecke der Welt auf. Dadurch fasziniert er sie. . . . Es verführt sie, Tolja als den 'Außergewöhnlichen' zu sehen, und eine neue Sehnsucht wird in ihr groß."[8]

However, this is a temporary experience for Yana. As she begins to see his lack of discipline and of a socialist consciousness, she returns to her collective and gives up her private world of which he has been the centre. "Ich hatte Tolja für außergewöhnlich gehalten, und plötzlich sah ich, er war banal" (p. 88), she observes. She realizes that he is the one who will have to change and grow in maturity; "Ich glaube, manche brauchen viel Zeit" (p. 6), she concludes. Nevertheless, although in the end the values of the socialist society are re-affirmed in Yana's decision to leave him, the outsider Tolja, with his aura of the exotic and unusual, plays, as the main character, a crucial role in the *Erzählung.*

Another *Erzählung* in which an exotic element surrounds the main character, an outsider, is Rudolf Bartsch's "Geisterbahn."[9] The protagonist consciously affirms his role as an outsider; he tells the business man, who shows a great interest in him: "Ich bin die Ausnahme. Sie sind die Regel" (p. 108). The two worlds which each represents are juxtaposed. The business man is fascinated by this exceptional person, who tells him: "Ich bin nicht einzuordnen, so ohne weiteres jedenfalls nicht. Ich bin in keinem Plan, in keiner Kartei, als eigenständiger Begriff nicht mal in Meyers Neuem Lexikon" (p. 102). He is a "ghost" in the house of horrors at the local amusement park. He observes:

---

[8] Plavius, "Gespräch mit Werner Heiduczek," p. 19.
[9] In *Prosa aus der DDR.*

In der Ausübung meines Berufs bin ich freier als jeder, der von einem der sogenannten
freien Berufe lebt ... Ich bin an keine Vorschriften gebunden, brauche mich dem
Geschmack der Konsumenten nicht anzupassen ... Mir redet keiner rein. (pp. 108–9)

His occupation as a "Vergnügungsgespenst" makes him not only an outsider,
but also lends him an aura of the exotic and unusual. Furthermore, the business
man senses a personal tragedy in this man's life, which adds to the fascination
which he has for him. The "ghost" is aware of this and tells him: "Das groteske
Unglück, das Sie hinter mir wittern, die originelle Misere, die ich in Ihren Augen
verkörpere, das gewisse Etwas, das sich in mir etabliert hat, das so ganz anders
ist als alles Herkömmliche. Das hat Sie angezogen" (p. 102). He is a man of
mystery, isolated from the rest of society, and as such he arouses the curiosity
of the business man, who, as a result persuades him to tell the story of his life.

The exotic element in "Geisterbahn" is used mainly by the author to create
an interest in his main character and to set the stage for the telling of the
protagonist's story. In the *Erzählungen Mark Aurel oder ein Semester
Zärtlichkeit* by Heiduczek and *Er kam mit dem Herbstwind* by Selber, it has
the function of revealing the conflict which may sometimes arise as a result of a
longing for the unusual and different by someone who is a member of a
community.

The "untypical" hero

In literary discussions of some *Erzählungen* of the GDR, the word
"untypical" (*untypisch*) is sometimes used to refer to the figure of the
outsider. It is used in contrast to the word *typisch,* which refers to the
"positive" hero of socialist realism. The outsider, who is untypical because he
does not fit in with the collective and the new society, is generally presented as
a negative figure.

According to the critic Alexander Abusch, the depiction of an isolated
individual who is not in harmony with his society is neither helpful nor
adequate in representing the goals and ideals of socialism. He states:

Ich möchte ... auf das Problem aufmerksam machen, daß die Position eines zu
"absonderlichen" Helden — als eines im ursprünglichen Sinne des Wortes sich
absondernden — die künstlerisch-ideelle Möglichkeit zur umfassenden Gestaltung der
Entwicklungsfragen unserer sozialistischen Gesellschaft außerordentlich einengt.[10]

Similarly, Klaus Jarmatz observes that in considering the depiction of the
outsider, the question that should be asked is "unter welchem Gesichtswinkel

---

[10] "Zu Werken unserer neueren erzählenden Literatur," in *Kritik in der Zeit,* p. 594.

so eine Gestalt angelegt ist, ob als gültiger Ausdruck des sozialistischen Menschenbildes oder als Figur, die in kritische Distanz gesetzt ist."[11] He adds: "Als Ausdruck für das sozialistische Menschenbild gibt diese Konstellation nichts her" (ibid.). Thus, to him the function of this figure in a work of literature is to depict a negative example.

However, Werner Heiduczek, the author of the *Erzählung Mark Aurel oder ein Semester Zärtlichkeit,* suggests that perhaps the outsider should not be labelled so quickly as a negative figure, as being *untypisch.* In an interview, he observes:

> Mir hat bis heute noch niemand glaubhaft definieren können, was denn nun eigentlich "typisch" ist. Ist "Ole Bienkopp" typisch oder nicht-typisch? Ich würde meinen beides. Das gerade macht ihn für mich zu einer einprägsamen Gestalt. Oft sehen wir einen Menschen nur als "Außenseiter" an, weil er nicht in das gewohnte – man könnte auch sagen "gewöhnliche" – Bild unserer Vorstellungen paßt.[12]

His character Tolja is untypical from the standpoint of socialist realism, but in terms of real life, Heiduczek is right in refusing to regard him as being entirely *untypisch.* An individual who does not fit into a mold, he attempts to find his own way through his difficulties. Yana, the heroine of the *Erzählung,* says that some persons need much time for their development: "Die müssen sich erst durchfressen, durch sich und das ganze Leben und überhaupt" (p. 6).

Heiduczek comments about his character:

> Ich würde mich gegen die Behauptung wehren, Tolja sei als Außenseiter konzipiert. Er gehört zu unserer Gesellschaft und in unsere Gesellschaft wie jede andere Gestalt aus dem Buch – nur ist er anders. . . . Eigenwillige Charaktere stempeln wir zu schnell und gedankenlos als Außenseiter ab. Wir disqualifizieren sie und geben ihnen den Teil der Schuld, den wir lieber auf uns nehmen sollten.[13]

Thus, for this author, the portrayal of the ideal is not the sole criterion, but rather the representation of an individual in his own right, even if he is a problematic one who does not fit in. However, Heiduczek's approach is an exception; the majority of stories of the GDR portray the ideal socialist.

As we have seen in this chapter, the figure of the outsider, as he is depicted in *Erzählungen* and *Kurzgeschichten,* shows a variety of approaches and intentions. In some narratives, he does represent a negative example, in others he changes, grows in maturity, and is absorbed by the collective, thus becoming a positive character. Sometimes he is associated with an exotic or romantic element that appears in the story.

---

[11] "Kritik in der Zeit," in *Kritik in der Zeit,* p. 77.
[12] Plavius, "Gespräch mit Werner Heiduczek," p. 19.
[13] Ibid., pp. 19–20.

Those writers who have portrayed the predicament of the old man who suddenly finds himself to be an outsider, or an "untypical" hero like Tolja, who has problems and cannot find an easy solution to them, show a concern for the individual and his particular problems in relating to the new society. They go beyond the stereotyped approach of presenting a perfect character, who is *typisch* in terms of socialist realism. They raise a question for which they apparently cannot provide an answer. This open question brings an element of uneasiness into the closed view of life which most stories present.

Chapter VI

THE HERO

The hero portrayed in the *Erzählungen* and *Kurzgeschichten* of the GDR incorporates the ideals of socialism. In the terminology of socialist realism, he is called the "positive" hero. He represents the new man of socialism, and as such he has the central place in its literature. Elisabeth Simons speaks of the new man, who is "der eigentliche ästhetische Gegenstand unserer Literatur,"[1] and Eva Strittmatter, in her essay "Literatur und Wirklichkeit," observes: "Die Bedeutung unserer Literatur wächst in dem Maße, wie es ihr gelingt, diesen neuen Helden zu profilieren."[2] The "positive" hero has grown around the figure of the worker and the revolutionary. According to Pracht and Neubert, socialist art did not truly begin until "Arbeiterrevolutionäre, die die Welt und sich selbst verändern, als neuer Heldentypus in die Kunst einzogen" (p. 154).

The new hero is an excellent worker, and his outstanding qualities and heroic achievements are closely linked with his work. He is a leader, and at the same time he is fully integrated with his collective. In everything he does he reveals *Parteilichkeit,* a socialist consciousness, and the desire to contribute towards the growth and development of the socialist society. It is in these attitudes, goals, and activities that he shows himself to be a modern socialist revolutionary. The *Kultur-Politisches Wörterbuch* says about him:

> Das neue Heldenbild der Literatur und Kunst der DDR entsteht insbesondere aus der Darstellung des Revolutionärs von heute, dessen revolutionäres Handeln der Gestaltung der entwickelten sozialistischen Gesellschaft und der Bewältigung der wissenschaftlich-technischen Revolution gilt. (p. 208)

He is confident and optimistic. A model and example to others, he is, at the same time, *volksverbunden,* that is, closely associated with, and expressing, the interests and concerns of the masses. He represents the ideal individual in the new society: the exemplary socialist in his relationship to work, the collective, himself and others, and in his role as a changer and builder of the society of the GDR.

Sometimes writers have tried to overcome the static quality of a perfect "positive" hero by portraying a protagonist with a character fault. However, this defect of character is never linked with his skill and responsibility as a worker, but rather with his private life and morals, and usually his fault is corrected before the story ends.

---

[1] " 'Das Andersmachen, von Grund auf,' " p. 193.
[2] In *Kritik in der Zeit,* p. 510.

The portrayal of the "Faustian" hero suggests another way of presenting movement and development in the figure of the "positive" hero. He keeps on striving as he faces various obstacles in his realization of socialist ideals. From a selfish, isolated individual, a "positive" hero emerges as, in the course of the narrative, he becomes actively involved in some form of work and a collective, and as he gains a socialist awareness.

The new hero is not presented as an individual in his own right, but as a representative of his class, possessing its best qualities. In that sense, the socialist hero is typical, and he is referred to as being "normal" and "ordinary," though, in fact, he is an ideal.

The worker as a hero

The literature of socialist realism draws its protagonists from the working class, because of a basic assumption of the kind of socialism to which the leadership of the GDR subscribes, that the true values and ideals of a society arise from this class. Pracht and Neubert state: "Die sozialistische Kunst reflektiert die neuen Wertvorstellungen, die sich aus der Lebenspraxis der revolutionären Arbeiterklasse ergeben . . ." (p. 156). The working class provides the values and ideals that go to make up the socialist view of man, and these are reflected in the literature of the new society.

An example of the true heroism of the labourer and his example to others, showing that true courage and values reside in him, is suggested by the *Kurzgeschichte* "Kurz nach Morgen"[3] by Manfred Jendryschik. The protagonist, a middle-aged lawyer, almost loses his grip on himself, and is unable to do his work properly, because of the depression caused by the sudden death of his wife. He hardly wants to get up in the morning. As a result of the following experience however, his attitude changes.

In handling the case of a 52-year-old carpenter who has lost his right arm in an accident, the lawyer asks the worker what he plans to do in his predicament. The man, after looking him up and down, suddenly shouts at him, his face red with anger: "So'n Quatsch, Mann! Sie haben wohl nie einen linkshändig arbeiten sehn, was? " (p. 191). The man's dauntless and unquestioning resolution to go on working gives the lawyer the courage and impetus to go on, too. This worker is the true hero of the *Kurzgeschichte,* though he only appears briefly.

Literary critics of the GDR frequently refer to the socialist hero as one who stands at the summit of his class and epoch.[4] He belongs to his class, is in

[3] In *Glas und Ahorn.*
[4] See, for example, Hans Jürgen Geerdts, "Einleitung," in *Literatur der DDR in Einzeldarstellungen,* p. XII; Uwe Kant, "Bräunigs gewöhnliche Geschichten," *NDL,* 17, No. 12 (1969), 147; Ursula Steinhaußen et al., *Handbuch für schreibende Arbeiter,* p. 150.

contact with it, but he is its most advanced and progressive representative. It is assumed that an ordinary worker in the midst of his labours is being shaped by his work in the direction of the socialist ideal, and that he is, therefore, the most suitable prototype for the hero of literature. This viewpoint is expressed, for example, by Walter Ulbricht at the First Bitterfeld Conference (1959): "Die Mitglieder der Brigaden, die täglich in den Produktionsbetrieben ihre Kraft und ihre Fähigkeiten . . . einsetzen, entwickeln sich zu den fortschrittlichsten Menschen, *zum Typ des sozialistischen Arbeiters.*"[5] Walter Ulbricht enjoined the writers of the GDR to look to these men for the models for their heroes. Pracht and Neubert also emphasize this view:

> Neue Wesenszüge sozialistischer Persönlichkeiten – das ist eine Lebenstatsache – entwickeln sich zuerst in der Arbeiterklasse. Es ist deshalb folgerichtig, daß Künstler, die ihre Vorstellung vom Menschenmöglichen bereichern und Entdecker von Neuem sein wollen, sich dem Lebensbereich zuwenden, in dem Neues entsteht. (p. 172)

Therefore, the writers of the GDR gave the figure of the socialist worker the central place in their works.

However, the kind of worker presented in their literary productions has changed, especially in narratives written after 1965. Whereas in the fifties and early sixties, writers portrayed individuals working in a factory or construction site, or farmers at an LPG, that is, workers involved in some kind of physical labour, in more recent *Erzählungen* and *Kurzgeschichten,* that is, those written in the late sixties and early seventies, they have presented highly trained executives or technical directors as their heroes. With the development of technology, the "technisch-wissenschaftliche Revolution," as it is referred to in the GDR, the image of the worker portrayed in literature has changed. In Volker Braun's *Erzählung Das ungezwungne Leben Kasts,* the hero began as a labourer, doing hard physical work. Later, he is portrayed as a student, and finally as a playwright, with the significant sidelight that he shows one of the actors how to hold a shovel properly on stage (p. 105).

In Benito Wogatzki's *Erzählungen* "Ein Tag und eine Nacht" and "Der Schmied und seine Frau,"[6] the protagonists are still ordinary workers, but in his story "Der Preis des Mädchens," the hero is an executive, which is also true of Siegfried Pitschmann's *Kurzgeschichte* "Der Direktor." The *Erzählung* "Fünf Versuche über Uwe"[7] by Pitschmann portrays a scientist. Erik Neutsch's "Drei Tage unseres Lebens" depicts a Party secretary, a mayor, and an architect, and Werner Bräunig's story with the programmatic title "Gewöhnliche Leute" an engineer. Though almost every walk of life is presented in these stories, an

---

[5] "Schlußwort zur 1. Bitterfelder Konferenz," in *Kritik in der Zeit,* p. 458.
[6] In *Der Preis des Mädchens.*
[7] In *Kontrapunkte.*

emphasis on the portrayal of persons associated with positions of leadership and intellectual pursuits is evident.

Walter Ulbricht's speech at the Second Bitterfeld Conference in 1964 set the pattern for this change in the literary depiction of the worker. He stated that the writer must learn to see things also from the vantage point of the planner and leader: "Er braucht unbedingt auch den Blickwinkel des Planers und Leiters."[8] Hella Dietz comments about Erik Neutsch, who wrote the *Erzählung* "Drei Tage unseres Lebens," showing the problems that challenge Party secretary Konz and Mayor Brüdering:

> Er zeigt, daß dabei Partei- und Staatsfunktionäre einen großen Packen Arbeit zu bewältigen haben. Die Erzählung vermittelt zumindest einen Schimmer davon, welches Maß an Kraft, politischem und fachlichem Wissen, Konzentration, Energie und Einfühlungsvermögen erforderlich ist, um Leitungstätigkeit verantwortlich ausüben zu können.[9]

But whether the hero of East German literature is a labourer or an executive, he still shows the qualities that mark the "positive" hero of socialist realism.

The "positive" hero

The "positive" hero, having arisen around the figure of the worker in a socialist society, is the model for the socialist man, wholly integrated with his collective, an exemplary worker and leader. He appears again and again in *Erzählungen* and *Kurzgeschichten,* recognizable by the characteristics which mark the socialist hero.

In Joachim Nowotny's *Erzählung* "Die Stunde nach der Prüfung,"[10] the youth Konrad finds the right kind of work for himself and reveals his newly acquired maturity. He passes his driver's test successfully and shows how keen and skillful he is at his newly found work: "Der Spund kam frisch von der Schulbank, setzte sich auf den Lanz und fuhr" (p. 215). He is optimistic and hopeful; he overcomes the discouragement that arises when others suggest that they may perhaps not need such a young tractor driver at the moment.

In his relationships with other people in the story, he shows himself dependable and helpful. He tries to help the old blacksmith, Kattun, and is polite to him, though Kattun has little use for the young upstart, as he calls him. Konrad overcomes the temptation to go into the pub to drink beer, even though a comrade tries to persuade him to do so; and to the two children

---

[8] "Über die Entwicklung einer volksverbundenen sozialistischen Nationalliteratur," in *Kritik in der Zeit*, p. 569.

[9] "Die Rede geht von uns," p. 179.

[10] In *Labyrinth ohne Schrecken.*

whom he meets quarrelling, he is an example and a friend. He shows his optimism and his progressive thinking when together they discuss how the LPG of their village will look some day when everything will be mechanized.

In Benito Wogatzki's *Erzählung* "Der Schmied und seine Frau" again, a worker is portrayed. An excellent blacksmith, strong and enthusiastic about his work, he is "ein Vorbild für alle" (p. 34), and earns a badge of merit. For twelve years he has been swinging his hammer; but when a new "Schmiede-maschine" is introduced, he is the first one to try it, because he is a progressive individual, who recognizes its significance for future technological develop-ment. He does not let a temporary setback discourage him, when he has to spend days and nights trying to make it work: "Er war der erste, der sie ausprobiert, der sie besiegt hatte. Es hatte Wochen gedauert. Niemand hatte sie eigentlich so recht gewollt" (p. 36). His own recent marriage is endangered because of the sacrifice of time and energy that is required until it works well. The smith is optimistic and confident and does not give up until he is successful.

In Benito Wogatzki's *Erzählung* "Der letzte Streich," Papa Kolbe is a leader and a hard worker. He is an example to Kurt Schemmel, whom he takes under his wing and guides to success in his work. Schemmel, who begins as a scrubber of vats in a factory, rises to become a leader and researcher who originates new ideas and methods of production. He is confident and optimistic, successful and, like his mentor, Papa Kolbe, concerned about the collective and the welfare of the workers.

In the *Kurzgeschichte* "Der Direktor," Siegfried Pitschmann presents a successful executive who is well liked by his collective, and who optimistically looks towards the future economic development of the GDR. Similarly, Party secretary Konz in Erik Neutsch's "Drei Tage unseres Lebens" is confident, has a high sense of duty and a socialist consciousness, and thinks of the future development of the town. He is a leader, an example to others, as well as a hard worker.

Many more examples can be added to this list. The protagonists of these *Erzählungen* and the *Kurzgeschichte* reveal the qualities which characterize the "positive" hero: he is an enthusiastic and excellent worker, is optimistic and successful, has a socialist consciousness, and is a leader involved in building up socialism. The "positive" hero is an example to others, completely affirming socialist values and ideals and acting in accordance with them. A literary critic, Horst Kieser, observes about Erik Neutsch's characters:

> Diese Gestalten sind meist kraftvolle, lebensprühende Kämpfernaturen, sozial klar determiniert; ihr sinnvolles Dasein wird auch in den exponiertesten Situationen nicht in Zweifel gezogen. Sie nehmen damit eine große Tradition auf, wie sie nur geschichtlich aufsteigende Klassen vorweisen können . . . [11]

[11] "Erik Neutsch," in *Literatur der DDR in Einzeldarstellungen*, p. 392.

With these words, he captures some of the qualities of the "positive" hero as he is portrayed not only by Erik Neutsch, but by other writers of the GDR.

In the *Handbuch für schreibende Arbeiter* a list of character traits that mark the "positive" hero are mentioned:

> Durch eine Reihe von Attributen wurde der 'sozialistische Held' im ethisch-moralischen Sinne charakterisiert: außergewöhnliche Persönlichkeit, menschliche Größe, Standhaftigkeit, Begeisterungsfähigkeit, Mut, Erlebnisfähigkeit, Parteilichkeit, Einfachheit, Willensstärke, Sichbekennenkönnen: Helden mit potenzierter geistiger und körperlicher Kraft und hervorragenden Charaktereigenschaften, die im Dienst der sozialistischen Gemeinschaft stehen.[12]

From this it can be seen that the "positive" hero is idealized to an extreme degree. The West German critic Gero von Wilpert defines him as "e. im positiven Sinne für die Interessen des Sozialismus handelnder . . . unkomplizierter und problemloser Held, als Verkörperung kommunistisch-revolutionären Heldentums stets 'typisch,' d.h. übertrieben idealisiert dargestellt . . ."[13]

Dealing with a stereotype

The "positive" heroes depicted in the *Erzählungen* and *Kurzgeschichten* of the GDR are exemplary characters, and as such they are perfect. Because of this, Hannes Stütz in Werner Bräunig's "Gewöhnliche Leute" does not need to change. He is successful and sure of himself, both in his work, in which he achieves all his goals and where he is a leader, and in his private life, when he meets and wins Adele. He overcomes all obstacles, has no inner problems, nor does he ever hesitate in anything. He is fully and happily integrated with his collective at the construction site. Some writers have found such a hero too stereotyped and too ideal. The lack of inner development and inner conflict in the protagonist, who is always positive and sure of himself, makes him appear stiff and uninteresting. The authors of the *Handbuch für schreibende Arbeiter* recognize this problem when they observe:

> Unter den 'positiven' Helden verstehen wir Helden, die vorwärtsdrängen und im Überwinden von Widersprüchen unsere Entwicklung vorantreiben helfen. Das notwendige Ideal des Autors, seinen Helden von einer hohen gesellschaftlichen Warte aus zu zeichnen, überlastete den Helden zuweilen mit einer Vollkommenheit, die ihn blutarm und statisch machte, ihm keine Entwicklungsmöglichkeiten gab. (p. 147)

---

[12] Steinhaußen et al., p. 146.
[13] *Sachwörterbuch der Literatur,* 5th ed., rev., Kröners Taschenausgabe, 231 (Stuttgart: Kröner, 1969), p. 584.

However, Bernhard Seeger affirms the concept of the "positive" hero. In spite of the dogmatic way in which he may sometimes have been presented, he insists that a hero of this dimension is needed as an example and ideal for the new society:

> Wir scheuen uns vor großen, starken Gestalten, weil es einmal eine unwissenschaftliche, unkünstlerische Auffassung vom positiven Helden gab. Diese Scheu – fürchte ich – wächst aus der Sorge, als Schönfärber zu gelten und in die Reihen der Dogmatiker verwiesen zu werden. Ich beharre nach wie vor auf dem Standpunkt, daß die Literatur die Gestalten in den Vordergrund rücken muß, die kraft ihrer Persönlichkeit befähigt sind, das Leben vorwärtszuentwickeln, Knoten zu lösen, Hindernisse niederzureißen, der Sache, wo sie zu Schaden gekommen ist, wieder zu ihrem echten Glanz zu verhelfen. Wir brauchen Helden, die die Macht ausüben und nicht erdulden.[14]

He implies that the example of such a hero portrayed in socialist literature would provide an incentive to achieve the goals of socialism.

Nevertheless, the writer is faced with a difficulty which becomes evident in the *Erzählungen*. Werner Bräunig has consistently portrayed the perfect hero, but in an already perfect society. Therefore, he is not out of place there, and is, in fact, one of many "positive" heroes. Other writers of short narrative prose have felt the need to add a negative quality to their hero to make him appear more natural. In Benito Wogatzki's *Erzählung* "Ein Tag und eine Nacht," Willi, the caterpillar operator, is presented as being an exceptionally skillful worker, but his morals and private life leave much to be desired. In Erik Neutsch's "Drei Tage unseres Lebens," Koblenz, a Party member and noted architect, has a morally corrupt son. The depiction of negative qualities in these characters is a device to give variety and colour to them. It usually does not affect the course of the story or the plot, and in most cases the individual remains a good socialist in spite of his fault. Furthermore, his character defect is usually corrected before the story ends.

In connection with the use of a character defect to lend colour to the hero, so that he does not appear static and anemic, the following fact can be observed in the narratives: the faults are invariably associated with the private life and morals of the character, rather than with his role as a worker in the new society. This suggests that the sphere of private morals is less important in socialism than the public role of the individual. Heinz Plavius observes this fact in his study of the "positive" hero, "Der positive Held im sozialistischen Realismus und der neue Charakter der Arbeit."[15] He says:

> In dem richtigen Bestreben nun, bei der Gestaltung des positiven Helden nicht in Schönfärberei zu verfallen und durch die rosarote Magie alle Probleme als gelöst

---

[14] Seeger, "Über den neuen Helden," in *Kritik in der Zeit*, p. 581.
[15] *Deutsche Zeitschrift für Philosophie*, 11, No. 8 (1963).

hinzustellen, erhalten die Helden eine Reihe negativer Charakterzüge und Eigenschaften. Das erwähnte Schema besteht darin, daß die Helden in ihrer Arbeit gute Leistungen vollbringen. Ihre negativen Eigenschaften aber beziehen sie sozusagen aus der Sphäre der Moral. (p. 953)

The "Faustian" hero

Heinz Plavius, in the same essay mentioned above, adds an important quality to his concept of the term, the "positive" hero, when he says about the protagonist of a certain story, that he is a "positive" hero, "weil er es unter komplizierten Umständen versteht, den richtigen Weg einzuschlagen" (p. 952). Plavius emphasizes the fact that, although this hero is not yet perfect, he is capable of changing himself. "Die Fähigkeit, bei der Veränderung seiner Umgebung sich selbst ständig zu verändern, ist das Hauptmerkmal des positiven Helden" (p. 954), he concludes. Plavius compares him to Faust: "Fausts geistiges Suchen und sein praktisches Streben sind gleichsam das Sinnbild dafür, daß diese Prozesse unendlich sind. Er irrte, strebte und fand immer neue Wahrheit bis an sein Ende" (p. 955).

An example, where this quality of striving is emphasized in the character of a hero, is found in Volker Braun's *Erzählung Das ungezwungne Leben Kasts*. Braun draws directly upon Goethe's *Faust* for symbols and metaphors to express his hero's restless striving. For example, a scene in this *Erzählung* is reminiscent of the "Osterspaziergang" in *Faust:* "Ich lief früh aus der dumpfen Behausung . . . Die Straßen füllten sich, ich wurde hineingezogen in den Strudel . . ." (p. 53). Kast is eager to experience life: "Ich wollte alles an mich heranlassen, oder es an mich reißen, was sich bot" (p. 54). Also the words of Faust spoken in the opening scene in his study are hinted at: "Bei mir nahm das Lernen kein Ende, die Bücher stapelten sich auf dem Fußboden, die Sätze und Seiten füllten den Kopf aus . . . Irgend etwas fehlte, vielleicht die alte Arbeit, ja, nur dahocken hier . . . Oder etwas anderes, was weiß ich" (ibid.).

The most telling comparison is made by the author in the scene where Kast is listening to a lecture on Goethe's *Urfaust* together with Linde, who later becomes a Gretchenfigure in the story. The point brought out is that Faust "will bindungsloser Mensch sein, will alles inbesitz nehmen! . . . Faust [ist] unfähig zu jeglicher Bindung" (pp. 59–60). This is a part of his nature and it causes Gretchen's tragedy, for she "vermag ihn nicht an sich zu binden" (p. 60). As Kast is following the lecture, he is observing Linde, so that the words of the lecture about Faust and Gretchen and his interaction with Linde become intertwined in a way which suggests how their relationship will develop, even though they have at this point just met: "Sie erscheint als Opfer dieser Unfähigkeit Fausts, tragisch . . . Ich sah ihren Nacken gebeugt, die Augen traurig, die Lippen schmal; sie schrieb etwas unter meine Zeilen — sie antwortet, sie sagt zu!" (ibid.)

At first Kast is completely involved with his love. He declares: "Ich war hingerissen von ihr, fühlte mich eins mit ihrem ganzen Wesen" (p. 62). But as she tries to bind him to herself and get married, especially after she is expecting a child, he feels more and more uneasy. He finally tells her that he cannot tie himself down by marrying her. They part, since she cannot live with him on his terms, but needs his commitment. The suggestion is made in the *Erzählung* that her desire to get married and settle down is bourgeois, and that, on the other hand, Kast's desire "aus freien Entschlüssen zu leben" (p. 101), as he puts it, is a quality which makes him a progressive member of the new society.

Though Kast does not want to commit himself to Linde, he is, at the same time, conscious of his growing loyalty to the collective. In terms of his work and active role in socialist society, he realizes that he must work together with others and commit himself to the collective. He says, for example, "es machte uns Spaß, viel von uns zu verlangen – und für Aufgaben zu leben, die uns immer mehr und mit *vielen* verbinden würden!" (p. 65). Throughout the story similar references occur, as, for example: "In der Gruppe bleiben. Es geht nur was zusammen" (p. 129). Shortly before he tells Linde that he cannot bind himself to her, he observes: "Ja, ich fühlte die Freude, mit vielen Freund zu sein, diese Freude würde ich nie verlieren aus der Brust" (p. 100). The process of his development is that from a personal relationship with one person, which he finds unsatisfactory and limiting, to a consciousness of being part of a larger whole, of the collective and of his society. Moreover, work takes a greater and greater precedence in his life. In a later love affair with Susanne, who is a more progressive socialist citizen than Linde, the lovers decide to set aside the selfish desire to lead a private life, and to part voluntarily for a while so that each can devote himself completely to his respective duties in the socialist society. In all this, Kast shows a growing realization and acceptance of the claims of socialism; this is the direction of his continuous striving and learning.

Like Faust, he goes on striving to the end in his endeavour to accomplish the task he has taken up. At the same time, he is a "positive" hero in his exemplary attitude towards work and his commitment to the collective. He learns to live his life more deeply in terms of socialist ideals and to sacrifice his private life. The impression of growth which the author tries to convey, that the protagonist is still on the road to socialist perfection, suggests a way of solving the problem of portraying a stiff and perfect hero.

The "typical" hero

The socialist hero, who stands for the man of the future, incorporates "eine aus der Wirklichkeit abgeleitete, klassenmäßige Vorstellung vom Menschen, wie er sein sollte – und sein *kann*" (Pracht and Neubert, p. 157). Thus, whether he is static and perfect, or a "Faustian" hero, who is developing in accordance with the ideal of socialism, the "positive" hero is a type, a model of perfection, based on the Marxist-Leninist ethos of the working class. He points to the future, to a " 'Wirklichkeit des morgigen Tages' (Plechanow)" (ibid.).

Maxim Gorki, who established the basic tenets of socialist realism, maintains that literature has a special task: "I want literature to rise above reality . . . It is not enough merely to depict already existing things — we must also bear in mind the things we desire and the things which are possible of achievement."[16] Thus, the literature of socialist realism depicts the ideals, the aims, and the vision of the future of socialism, and the protagonist of such a work is not an ordinary person, but one who exemplifies the characteristic attributes of the "positive" hero. What is important, therefore, are the ideas portrayed by the character, rather than the depiction of a particular human being. He becomes a representative of a larger entity, a class; he becomes a type. Thus, from the point of view of socialist realism, the word "typical" has been given a new meaning. It means presenting something ideal as if it possessed concrete reality. The West German critic Lothar von Balluseck observes:

> Es gehört dialektischer Scharfsinn dazu, um das in unserem Sinne Untypische als typisch zu begreifen. Ein Brigadier, ein Aktivist können nicht negativ gezeichnet werden in einem Werk, das Anspruch auf 'typische Wiedergabe' erhebt, da für die Träger fortschrittlicher Verhaltensweisen auch im menschlichen Bereich gute Eigenschaften charakteristisch sein müssen. Die Herausarbeitung dieser guten Eigenschaften, ihre bewußte Betonung, ja, Übertreibung entspricht den Gesetzen der Parteilichkeit und ist daher zu bejahen. . . . So hat Gorki einmal gesagt, daß die 'wahre Kunst das Recht der Übertreibung genießt.'[17]

It is this view of literature which, for example, permits Siegfried Pitschmann to refer to his hero Uwe in the *Erzählung* "Fünf Versuche über Uwe" as "der klassische Fall einer normalen Entwicklung, allein möglich unter modernen Verhältnissen wie den unseren . . ." (p. 198). Uwe is typical or normal in the sense of being the representative of the socialist ideal, but throughout the story he is presented as someone special, as being unusually gifted and exemplary. The young scientist is an individual who occupies the place of a hero in his society. His professor comments: "Das ist er, der mir auffiel schon zu Beginn der agrarbiologischen Unterrichtung . . . die er gar nicht nötig hatte zu hören laut Plan, wo er freiwillig noch abends im Labor hockte . . ." (p. 196). He is ambitious and devoted to his work. The professor adds that he found him to be "maßlos unbescheiden, soll heißen, in seiner Wißbegier, seinem Erkenntnistrieb . . . (ibid.), and speaks of his quick mind and skillful hands, "sogar das Sezieren wird so zum ästhetischen Anblick" (p. 197).

---

[16] *Literature and Life* (London: Hutchinson International Authors, 1946), p. 145.
[17] *Dichter im Dienst* (Wiesbaden: Limes, 1963), p. 22.

His wife remarks, that he is one "den du erkennen sollst an seiner Verläßlichkeit, dem sicheren Beruhen ... der Gelehrte von morgen, der große Erklärer ... dem alles einfach erscheint ..." (p. 181). Thus, Uwe is an exceptional individual in every way; but, when his wife speaks of their life together, she observes: "Ich würde aber nicht von Idealen reden; du sollst uns lieber als Normalfall sehen" (p. 183).

Though Siegfried Pitschmann's hero is exceptional, the word "Normalfall" is used in referring to him. This fact suggests, that the word "normal," as used by the author, refers to a perfect hero of socialist realism. He is the standard and the measure of the way the individual in the new society should be, and will be, in the future. Hence, he is "typical" in the socialist sense of the word.

On the other hand, the individual in his own right, as a private person, represents the abnormal one. Hans Joachim Bernhard, in "Normalfälle,"[18] his review of Siegfried Pitschmann's stories, brings out this contrast, when he states:

> Pitschmann wendet sich nicht dem Abseitigen, dem Sonderfall zu, es geht ihm nicht um die literarische 'Rettung' des Peripheren. Es sind Grundfragen unseres Lebens, der Entwicklung der sozialistischen Menschengemeinschaft, die er aufwirft ... Nicht der Außenseiter mit der fragwürdigen Interessantheit seines Schicksals, sondern 'Normalfälle' werden erhellt, der Mut, die Ausdauer, die Menschenfreundlichkeit, die ein solches 'normales' Leben in der und für die sozialistische Gemeinschaft ... ausmachen. Die Konzeption der genannten Geschichten erlaubt es, das 'Normale' in relativer thematischer Breite und in wichtigen Phasen seiner Genesis vorzuführen. (p. 182)

Thus, the word "normal" means that which is consistent with socialism, with the new society, and, more than that, with the ideal itself, rather than with anything that is average or usual in every-day life. The ideal becomes the standard. Hans Joachim Bernhard defines "normal" in the following way:

> Normal: das heißt nicht, durchschnittlich oder selbstzufrieden, heißt nicht ein Lebensweg ohne Konflikte und persönliches Versagen im Einzelfall. Normal: das ist der Wille zu verändern, das überlegte Ungestüm, die hohen Forderungen an sich selbst. Es ist das Normale in einer 'modernen Gesellschaft wie der unseren.' (p. 184)

With these words he describes at the same time the ideal of the "positive" hero and his relationship to the socialist society.

In a similar way, the word "gewöhnlich" is used to refer to the typical hero. An example of this is the title of Werner Bräunig's *Erzählung* "Gewöhnliche Leute." Though Bräunig's heroes are called "gewöhnlich," they are in fact extraordinary. In his review "Bräunigs gewöhnliche Geschichten,"[19] Uwe Kant comments:

[18] *NDL,* 17, No. 3 (1969).
[19] *NDL,* 17, No. 12 (1969).

Bräunigs Helden . . . sind schon Riesen . . . Aber es sind keine Riesen, zu denen die
Menge staunend emporglotzen muß. Sie sind nicht das Unmaß, sondern das Maß. Sie
sind erreichbar noch in der Epoche, weil sie ihr nicht voraus sind, sondern auf ihrer
Höhe. Und schon ein paar hundert Meter weiter gibt es mehr von ihnen, etwa
Sandmann vom Schulbau oder Moßmann, den Brückenbauer. . . . Sie sehen sich selbst
so sicher und selbstverständlich, so unerschüttert durch das Leben gehen, sie sind so
sehr auf der Hochebene . . . (pp. 146–47)

The word "gewöhnlich" is used by Bräunig in a relative sense, that is, it does
not yet apply to the common experience, but it will in the future, because of
the particular development of society. This process is inevitable according to
socialist doctrine, and, therefore, one can already speak of the heroes of
socialism, who are at the forefront of this development, as being "ordinary."
Volker Ebersbach sums up this concept when he says: "Das Ungewöhnliche
von heute wird als das Normale von morgen dargestellt . . ."[20] It is this view of
the hero which makes it possible for Werner Bräunig to name his story of
Hannes Stütz and Adele Noth "Gewöhnliche Leute," even though they are
extraordinary, and Siegfried Pitschmann to call the life of his hero Uwe
"normal," even though it is exceptional.

[20] "Benito Wogatzki: Der Preis des Mädchens," *WB*, 18, No. 9 (1972), p. 156.

CONCLUSION

The present study has examined a selection of representative *Erzählungen* and *Kurzgeschichten* written in the GDR between 1965 and 1972. These prose narratives deal mainly with the individual in the new society, portraying his relationship to his work, to his collective, and to his family, and revealing his attitude and commitment to the aims and ideals of a socialist society. Moreover, they show that work and the collective constitute the two central aspects of his life.

Work is an activity which affects, influences, and shapes every aspect of the individual's life. The protagonist is very often a member of the working class, and he is usually presented in connection with some useful work; also, the setting of the narratives is usually a place where work is done: a construction site, a factory. The female characters are almost without exception engaged in some type of work or a profession outside the home. The few minor characters who do not work are decadent and immoral.

Work transforms the individual, enabling him to break through his isolation and to become integrated with the community of workers and with the rest of society. It helps him to find meaning and fulfillment and to realize his true potential. Most important of all, it develops his socialist consciousness. A new kind of morality, an *Arbeitsmoral,* connected with his responsibility at work, also becomes apparent. Socialist labour is seen as a shaping and moral force in man. Its aim is to become the central activity in his life: "das erste Lebensbedürfnis" (Marx).

United by a common task and sharing the same experience of work, a community of workers, the collective, comes into being. It has an organic unity and it provides the ideal setting for work. All members are needed, all co-operate. A task is achieved more quickly and efficiently by a collective. It multiplies the individual's resources; through the concerted effort of all its members, the seemingly impossible is achieved.

But more than just being the setting for work, the collective is a vital social unit in the new society. Especially Werner Bräunig's *Erzählungen* emphasize how work unites individuals. Social differences are absent; all meet on an equal basis. Newcomers quickly feel at home. The collective gives each person a sense of identity and of belonging to a group. Personal relationships like love and marriage are dependent on, and influenced by, this community of workers. An ideal marriage partnership is possible when both members are integrated with the collective, possess a socialist consciousness, and have a trade or profession in which both are successful. Work and the collective thus form the basis of a stable relationship. If one of the partners lacks a socialist consciousness and is not in harmony with the community, then the relationship does not have a sufficient basis. In that case, the more progressive member frequently leaves the lover and chooses in favour of the collective.

The readiness of a person to participate in the life of a collective depends on his maturity, that is, the degree to which his socialist consciousness has been developed, which, in turn, is determined by his commitment to, and involvement in, his work. Thus work is the source of the socialist personality, and the collective is the setting in which it can express itself most fully.

Closely associated with the socialist maturity of the individual within the collective is his responsibility to it. He must not only think of himself when he makes a choice, but must also consider the welfare of the other members of his community. The person who has a position of leadership, as, for example, a brigadier, has an additional responsibility towards each of the workers. The collective, in turn, has a duty to its members. It corrects and reprimands where necessary; it encourages workers to do better work.

The leader is ahead of the others in the development of his socialist consciousness; he is a pacemaker (*Schrittmacher*), yet he is also the individual most fully in harmony with his group. This progressive leader, the "positive" hero of socialist realism, represents the ideal. He is an excellent worker; his outstanding qualities and heroic achievements are closely linked with his work. He is optimistic and confident. He reveals a socialist consciousness, a commitment to socialist ideals, a concern for the welfare of the collective, and a desire to contribute towards the growth and development of the socialist society. A model and example to others, he is at the same time closely associated with the interests of the masses. The "positive" hero is the product of socialism, and, as such, he becomes a representative of a larger entity, a class. He becomes a type; he is the standard and measure of the way every individual in a socialist society should be, and will be, in the future. Therefore, he is referred to in the stories as being normal and ordinary.

This new man of socialism is both the product and the mover, the object and the subject of socialist historical progress. As he is being shaped according to socialist ideals and aims, he can influence and shape others in turn. He is therefore able to bring about change in society, both by his example and his efforts. He guides other workers to develop their skills and to further their education, and he encourages them to contribute their ideas in achieving social, industrial, and economic improvements. A man of vision, who sees the present in terms of the ideal future, he awakens enthusiasm in others. Often presented as a skillful scientist or executive, he helps to further technological and economic progress.

However, not only the leader with a well-developed socialist consciousness, but each individual is encouraged to do his share in bringing about socialist change. Thus, in some stories, the simple and honest worker, a naive socialist, contributes towards social improvement. Holding an office or a position of influence is not necessary, because change should come spontaneously from the working class. What is important is taking the initiative and beginning to change what needs to be changed. Each person has the responsibility to choose and to make use of all the possibilities set before him to bring about and further socialist change and the economic production of the GDR.

Many stories deal particularly with the role of women in the new society. These narratives reveal most dramatically the shift from traditional ways of thinking to those which characterize socialism. They show most clearly the effect of work, the meaning and importance of the collective and the extent of the revolutionary changes in society and in technology which have occurred in the GDR.

The women in the *Erzählungen* and *Kurzgeschichten* stand out as the progressive individuals in contrast to the men in their lives, who frequently show remnants of bourgeois thinking. The women are *bewußt,* capable, successfull, have a socialist personality, and incorporate in their attitude to life and society the ideals of socialism. They are often presented as taking the lead in unselfish action, in making personal choices according to socialist ideals, in moving away from a world of private happiness to take an active role in the working world. The careers which they choose are often connected with science or the area of machinery.

The woman's career is more important than her marriage or love relationship. If a husband or lover is backward, as is often the case in the stories, conflict is created. Often the woman has to leave him and find her own way. She chooses the more difficult road of independence, of working unselfishly for the good of her society, rather than allowing herself to be taken care of by a husband or lover.

The collective assumes a primary value in the life and relationships of most of the individuals portrayed in the stories. The movement towards integration with the collective is the most striking feature of the *Erzählungen* and *Kurzgeschichten* of the GDR. The individual takes the step "vom Ich zum Wir." Overcoming his isolation and self-centredness, he moves towards greater and greater unity and integration with the community of workers.

As a person identifies more and more with the interests of the group, family ties and personal relationships begin to recede into the background. Loyalty to the collective takes precedence over family ties, and the interests of the group become the individual's personal concern.

In the portrayal of the "Faustian" hero, who keeps on striving, the trend towards the collective is paramount. The direction of his continuous striving and learning is a growing loyalty and commitment to the group. The importance of the collective is also revealed by the fact that when a writer wants to give variety and colour to the stereotyped "positive" hero, he adds a character defect that is associated with the private life and morals of a man, rather than with his role as a worker in the new society. This suggests that in socialism the sphere of private morals is less important than the individual's public role. The chief values are those of the community of workers and those qualities which make a person a desirable member of it.

The power of the collective, as it is presented in the stories, also becomes evident in the portrayal of the outsider, the individual who does not fit in. He is either presented as a negative example to be eschewed, or as someone who must change by gaining insight and a socialist awareness. The community has the strength within itself to educate and integrate the rootless and undecided person who is outside it. The outsider has to be either excluded or converted. Diverse opinions do not fit in; they mar the ideal which these narratives present.

The general impression that these *Erzählungen* and *Kurzgeschichten* give is that of success and optimism. The individual is valued because of his contribution to the collective and his ability to work. Only the successful and optimistic person who is integrated with the collective and skillful in his work has a place in the new society. The supreme values according to the stories are the ability to work, strength, power, progress, and increased economic production. Helplessness, old age, disability, and death have no place in the socialist society presented in these narratives. Thus, an ideal world and society are presented by the majority of writers in their short narrative prose works written between 1965 and 1972. Their purpose is to educate in a particular direction. The world is seen as a socialist would wish to see it, and unpleasant aspects are ignored. A closed view of life is presented in most stories. They depict the ideals, the aims, and the vision of the future of socialism.

SELECTED BIBLIOGRAPHY

A. *Primary Sources:*

Anderle, Hans Peter, ed. *Mitteldeutsche Erzähler: Eine Studie mit Proben und Porträts.* Köln: Verlag Wissenschaft und Politik, 1965.
Auf einer Straße: Zehn Geschichten. bb [Taschenbücher], 194. Berlin: Aufbau-Verlag, 1968.
Bieler, Manfred. *Märchen und Zeitungen.* Berlin: Aufbau-Verlag, 1966.
Bitterfelder Ernte: Eine Anthologie schreibender Arbeiter des Bezirkes Halle, 1959–1967. Ed. Bezirksvorstand des FDGB Halle und der Rat des Bezirkes Halle. Berlin: Verlag Tribüne, 1968.
Boas, Horst. *Die Botschaft: Erzählungen und Skizzen.* Berlin: Union Verlag, 1962.
Bobrowski, Johannes. *Mäusefest und andere Erzählungen.* Quarthefte 3. Berlin: Wagenbach, 1966.
– *Der Mahner: Erzählungen und andere Prosa aus dem Nachlaß.* Quarthefte 29. Berlin: Wagenbach, 1968.
Borchert, Christa. *Bedrohung der Stadt Bor: Erzählungen.* Berlin: Verlag der Nation, 1967.
Bradatsch, Gertrud. *Spiegelmacher: Erzählungen.* Rostock: Hinstorff, 1970.
Bräunig, Werner. *Gewöhnliche Leute: Sieben Erzählungen.* Halle/Saale: Mitteldeutscher Verlag, 1971.
Braun, Günter und Johanna. *Die Nase des Neandertalers: Kurzgeschichten.* Berlin: Verlag Neues Leben, 1969.
Braun, Volker. *Das ungezwungne Leben Kasts.* Edition Neue Texte. Berlin: Aufbau-Verlag, 1972.
Brenner, Hildegard, ed. *Nachrichten aus Deutschland: Eine Anthologie der neueren DDR-Literatur.* Reinbek bei Hamburg: Rowohlt, 1967.
Brězan, Jurij. *Der Mäuseturm.* Berlin: Verlag Neues Leben, 1970.
– *Reise nach Krakau: Erzählung.* Roman für alle, 201. Berlin: Verlag der Nation. 1970.
Brokerhoff, Karl Heinz, ed. *DDR-Literatur VI: Lyrik; Prosa; Drama/Hörspiel.* Literatur aus dem anderen Teil Deutschlands, Textsammlungen für den Unterricht, vol. 6. Bonn-Bad Godesberg: Hohwacht, 1971.
– *Geschichten von Drüben II: Erzählungen und Kurzgeschichten aus dem anderen Teil Deutschlands.* Textsammlungen für den Unterricht, vol. 4. Bad Godesberg: Hohwacht, 1968.
Bruyn, Günter de. *Hochzeit in Weltzow: Erzählungen.* Reclams Universal-Bibliothek, 407. Leipzig: Reclam, 1968.
– *Ein schwarzer, abgrundtiefer See: Erzählungen.* Halle/Saale: Mitteldeutscher Verlag, 1963.
Floß, Rolf. *Irina.* 3rd ed. Halle/Saale: Mitteldeutscher Verlag. 1970.
Fries, Fritz Rudolf. *Der Fernsehkrieg: Erzählungen.* Halle/Saale: Mitteldeutscher Verlag, 1969.
Fühmann, Franz. *Der Jongleur im Kino oder Die Insel der Träume.* Rostock: Hinstorff, 1970.
– *Das Judenauto: Vierzehn Tage aus zwei Jahrzehnten.* Zürich: Diogenes, 1968.
– *König Ödipus: Gesammelte Erzählungen.* 2nd ed. Berlin: Aufbau-Verlag, 1968.
Geschichten. Ed. Kollektiv Eulenspiegel Verlag. Eulenspiegels Neue Vortragsbücher. 3rd ed., rev. Berlin: Eulenspiegel, 1967.
Heiduczek, Werner. *Mark Aurel oder ein Semester Zärtlichkeit.* 2nd ed. Berlin: Verlag Neues Leben, 1972.

Heinrich, Helmut T. *Hölderlin auf dem Wege von Bordeaux: Erzählungen.* Edition Neue Texte. Berlin: Aufbau-Verlag, 1971.

Hermlin, Stephan. *Gedichte und Prosa.* Berlin: Wagenbach, 1965.

− *Reise eines Malers in Paris: Erzählung.* Leipzig: Insel, 1966.

− *Die Zeit der Gemeinsamkeit. In einer dunklen Welt: Zwei Erzählungen.* Quarthefte 16. Berlin: Wagenbach, 1966.

Hofmann, Fritz. *Die Erbschaft des Generals.* Edition Neue Texte. Berlin: Aufbau-Verlag, 1972.

Ich schreibe . . . : Arbeiter greifen zur Feder. Vols. 1−4. Berlin-Treptow: Verlag Tribüne, and Halle/Saale: Mitteldeutscher Verlag, 1960−64.

Im Strom der Zeit: Erzählungen. Halle/Saale: Mitteldeutscher Verlag, 1965.

Jakobs, Karl-Heinz. *Beschreibung eines Sommers: Roman.* 2nd ed. Berlin: Verlag Neues Leben, 1962.

− *Merkwürdige Landschaften: Sieben ausgewählte Geschichten.* Halle/Saale: Mitteldeutscher Verlag, 1964.

− *Eine Pyramide für mich: Roman.* Berlin: Verlag Neues Leben, 1971.

Jendryschik, Manfred, ed. *Bettina pflückt wilde Narzissen: 66 Geschichten von 44 Autoren.* Halle/Saale: Mitteldeutscher Verlag, 1972.

− *Die Fackel und der Bart: Dreiunddreißig Geschichten.* Rostock: Hinstorff, 1971.

− *Glas und Ahorn: Achtundzwanzig Geschichten.* Rostock: Hinstorff, 1967.

Joho, Wolfgang. *Abschied von Parler.* Edition Neue Texte. Berlin: Aufbau-Verlag, 1972.

Kant, Hermann. *Die Aula: Roman.* Berlin: Rütten and Loening, 1965.

− *Ein bißchen Südsee: Erzählungen.* München: dtv 679, 1970.

− *Das Impressum: Roman.* Berlin: Rütten and Loening, 1972.

Köhler, Erich. *Nils Harland: Erzählungen.* Rostock: Hinstorff, 1968.

Korall, Harald and Werner Liersch, eds. *Erfahrungen: Erzähler der DDR: Anthologie.* Halle/Saale: Mitteldeutscher Verlag, 1969.

Korall, Harald. *Hochzeit nach neun Jahren: Erzählungen.* Halle/Saale: Mitteldeutscher Verlag, 1970.

− ed. *Literatur 71: Almanach.* Halle/Saale: Mitteldeutscher Verlag, 1971.

Kraze, Hanna-Heide. *Steinchen schmeißen: Kindergeschichten für Erwachsene.* 3rd ed. Berlin: Union Verlag, 1971.

Kunert, Günter. *Die Beerdigung findet in aller Stille statt: Erzählungen.* Reihe Hanser, 11. 4th ed. München: Hanser, 1970.

− *Betonformen. Ortsangaben.* Berlin: Literarisches Colloquium, 1969.

− *Im Namen der Hüte: Roman.* München: Hanser, 1967.

− *Kramen in Fächern: Geschichten, Parabeln, Merkmale.* 2nd ed. Berlin: Aufbau-Verlag, 1972.

− *Ortsangaben.* Edition Neue Texte. Berlin: Aufbau-Verlag, 1971.

− *Tagträume in Berlin und andernorts: Kleine Prosa, Erzählungen, Aufsätze.* München: Hanser, 1972.

Laabs, Joochen. "Der Weichenreiniger." *Neue Deutsche Literatur,* 15, No. 9 (1967), 138−44.

Landung auf Paradies-Ort: Liebesgeschichten. Berlin: Buchverlag Der Morgen, 1971.

Lenz, Werner. *Post aus Südamerika: Erzählungen.* Halle/Saale: Mitteldeutscher Verlag, 1972.

Morgner, Irmtraud. *Gauklerlegende: Eine Spielfraungeschichte.* Berlin: Eulenspiegel, 1970.

− *Hochzeit in Konstantinopel.* 2nd ed. Berlin: Aufbau-Verlag, 1970.

Nachbar, Herbert. *Die Millionen des Knut Brümmer.* 2nd ed. Rostock: Hinstorff, 1971.

Neue Texte: Almanach für deutsche Literatur. 2 vols. Berlin: Aufbau-Verlag, 1967−68.

Neutsch, Erik. *Bitterfelder Geschichten.* Halle/Saale: Mitteldeutscher Verlag, 1961.

− *Die anderen und ich.* Halle/Saale: Mitteldeutscher Verlag, 1970.

Noglik, Gerd, ed. *Voranmeldung.* Halle/Saale: Mitteldeutscher Verlag, 1968.

Nowotny, Joachim. *Labyrinth ohne Schrecken: Erzählungen.* Halle/Saale: Mitteldeutscher Verlag, 1967.

— *Sonntag unter Leuten: Erzählungen.* Halle/Saale: Mitteldeutscher Verlag, 1971.

Das Paar: 13 Liebesgeschichten. bb [Taschenbücher] 238. Berlin: Aufbau-Verlag, 1971.

Pitschmann, Siegfried. *Kontrapunkte: Geschichten und kurze Geschichten.* Berlin: Aufbau-Verlag, 1968.

Plenzdorf, Ulrich. "Die neuen Leiden des jungen W." *Sinn und Form,* 24, No. 2 (1972), 254–310.

Ret, Joachim, Achim Roscher, Heinz Sachs, eds. *Manuskripte: Almanach Neuer Prosa und Lyrik.* Halle/Saale: Mitteldeutscher Verlag, 1969.

Richter, Egon. *Ferien am Feuer.* Frankfurt am Main: Röderberg-Verlag, 1966.

Rühlicke, Horst. *Das elfte Jahr: Erzählungen.* Berlin: Union Verlag, 1964.

Sachs, Heinz, ed. *Die die Träume vollenden: Fünf moderne Erzählungen.* Halle/Saale: Mitteldeutscher Verlag, 1969.

Sakowski, Helmut. *Zwei Zentner Leichtigkeit: Geschichten.* 2nd ed. Berlin: Verlag Neues Leben, 1971.

Schmidt, Joachim, ed. *Begegnung: Anthologie neuer Erzähler.* Rostock: Hinstorff, 1969.

Schmitt, Hans-Jürgen, ed. *Neunzehn Erzähler der DDR.* Fischer Taschenbuch, 1210. Frankfurt am Main: Fischer, 1971.

Schneider, Rolf. *Brücken und Gitter: Ein Vorspruch und sieben Geschichten.* München: Piper, 1965.

Schütz, Helga. *Das Erdbeben bei Sangerhausen und andere Geschichten.* Berlin: Aufbau-Verlag, 1972.

— *Vorgeschichten oder Schöne Gegend Probstein.* Edition Neue Texte. Berlin: Aufbau-Verlag, 1971.

Seghers, Anna. *Aufstand der Fischer von St. Barbara.* Bibliothek Suhrkamp, 20. [Frankfurt am Main]: Suhrkamp, 1966.

— *Geschichten aus Mexiko.* Berlin: Aufbau-Verlag, 1970.

— *Die Kraft der Schwachen.* Berlin: Aufbau-Verlag. 1966.

— "Sagen von Unirdischen." *Sinn und Form,* 24 (1972), 16–40.

— *Überfahrt: Eine Liebesgeschichte.* Berlin: Aufbau-Verlag, 1971.

Selber, Martin. *Er kam mit dem Herbstwind: Erzählung.* 3rd ed. Halle/Saale: Mitteldeutscher Verlag, 1970.

Specht, Joachim. *Stippvisite und andere Erzählungen.* Berlin: Verlag der Nation, 1968.

Stade, Martin. *Der himmelblaue Zeppelin: Erzählungen.* Halle/Saale: Mitteldeutscher Verlag, 1970.

Strittmatter, Erwin. *Ein Dienstag im September: 16 Romane im Stenogramm.* Berlin: Aufbau-Verlag, 1969.

— *3/4 hundert Kleingeschichten.* Edition Neue Texte. Berlin: Aufbau-Verlag, 1971.

— *Ole Bienkopp: Roman.* Berlin: Aufbau-Verlag, 1972.

— *Schulzenhofer Kramkalender.* 4th ed. Berlin: Aufbau-Verlag, 1971.

Der Tag hat 24 Stunden: Eine Anthologie des Zirkels schreibender Arbeiter im VEB Petrolchemisches Kombinat Schwedt. Berlin: Verlag Tribüne, 1971.

Unterdörfer, Gottfried. *Von Abend zu Abend: Neun Liebesgeschichten.* 2nd ed. Berlin: Union Verlag, 1967.

Verflixte Gedanken: Prosa schreibender Arbeiter. Ed. Hans Schmidt, Wolfgang Himmelreich, Anita Baldauf. Berlin: Verlag Tribüne, 1970.

Die vierte Laterne: Voranmeldung: Anthologie. Ed. Joachim Schmidt et al. Halle/Saale: Mitteldeutscher Verlag, 1971.

Walther, Klaus, ed. *Mit Ehrwürden fing alles an: Neun heitere Geschichten.* 2nd ed. Halle/Saale: Mitteldeutscher Verlag, 1970.

Walwei-Wiegelmann, Hedwig, ed. *Ohne Bilanz und andere Prosa aus der DDR.* Sein und Sagen, Texte für den Deutschunterricht, Heft 16. 2nd ed. Frankfurt am Main: Hirschgraben-Verlag, 1971.

— *Prosa aus der DDR.* Paderborn: Schöningh, 1969.

Weinert, Gerda. *Ein Schritt vor die Tür: Kurze Geschichten.* Rostock: Hinstorff, 1969.

Wenzel, Karl-Heinz, Marianne Schmidt, Konrad Schmidt, eds. *Körnchen Gold: Eine Anthologie schreibender Arbeiter.* Berlin: Verlag Tribüne, 1969.

Wie der Kraftfahrer Karli Birnbaum seinen Chef erkannte: Neue Prosa – Neue Namen. Berlin: Verlag Neues Leben, 1971.

Wie Nickel zweimal ein Däne war: Neue Prosa – Neue Namen. Berlin: Verlag Neues Leben, 1970.

Wogatzki, Benito. "Am anderen Ufer: Erzählung." *Neue Deutsche Literatur,* 19, No. 12 (1971), 17–52.

— "Christine." *Sinn und Form,* 24 (1972) 142–65.

— "Der Mann aus dem Kessel." *Sinn und Form,* 22 (1970), 1344–55.

— *Der Preis des Mädchens.* Berlin: Verlag Neues Leben, 1971.

— "Die Wichelsbacher Initiative." *Sinn und Form,* 22 (1970), 1078–94.

Wolf, Christa. *Der geteilte Himmel: Erzählung.* 3rd ed. Halle/Saale: Mitteldeutscher Verlag, 1963.

— *Nachdenken über Christa T.* Sammlung Luchterhand, 31. Neuwied: Luchterhand, 1971.

Wolff, Lutz-W., ed. *Fahrt mit der S-Bahn: Erzähler der DDR.* München: DTV 778, 1971.

Zeitzeichen: Prosa vom Tage. Berlin: Buchverlag Der Morgen, [19]68.

Zirkel schreibender Arbeiter BKW "Erich Weinert," Deuben, Kreis Hohenmölsen. *Deubener Blätter.* Vol. 2. Halle/Saale: Mitteldeutscher Verlag, 1964.

Zwischenprüfung für Turandot: Geschichten und Gedichte. Ed. Ute Fichtner, Hans-Georg Lietz, Ingrid Prignitz. Rostock: Hinstorff, 1970.

B. Secondary Sources:

Abusch, Alexander. *Literatur im Zeitalter des Sozialismus: Beiträge zur Literaturgeschichte 1921 bis 1966.* Berlin: Aufbau-Verlag, 1967.

Albrecht, Günter et al. *Lexikon deutschsprachiger Schriftsteller von den Anfängen bis zur Gegenwart.* 2 vols. Leipzig: Bibliographisches Institut, 1967–68.

Apel, Hans. *DDR 1962, 1964, 1966.* Berlin: Voltaire, 1967.

Balluseck, Lothar von. *Dichter im Dienst: Der sozialistische Realismus in der deutschen Literatur.* 2nd ed. Wiesbaden: Limes, 1963.

— *Literatur und Ideologie 1963: Zu den literaturpolitischen Auseinandersetzungen seit dem VI. Parteitag der SED.* Bad Godesberg. Hohwacht, 1963.

Baum, Werner. *Bedeutung und Gestalt: Über die sozialistische Novelle.* Halle/Saale: Mitteldeutscher Verlag, 1968.

Bernhard, Hans Joachim. "Normalfälle." Rev. of *Kontrapunkte: Geschichten und kurze Geschichten,* by Siegfried Pitschmann. *Neue Deutsche Literatur,* 17, No. 3 (1969), 178–84.

Bilke, Jörg Bernhard. "Auf den Spuren der Wirklichkeit: DDR-Literatur: Traditionen, Tendenzen, Möglichkeiten." *Der Deutschunterricht,* 21, No. 5 (1969), 24–60.

— "Planziel Literaturgesellschaft oder Gibt es zwei deutsche Literaturen? " *Aus Politik und Zeitgeschichte: Beilage zur Wochenzeitung Das Parlament,* 18 Dec. 1971, pp. 3–37.

Bittighöfer, Bernd and Jürgen Schmollack, eds. *Moral und Gesellschaft: Entwicklungsprobleme der sozialistischen Moral in der DDR.* Berlin: Dietz, 1968.

Bock, Sigrid. "Nachdenken über die Kraft der Liebe . . . : Zur Erzählung 'Überfahrt' von Anna Seghers." *Sinn und Form,* 23 (1971), 1353–57.

— "Neuer Gegenstand — neues Erzählen." *Weimarer Beiträge,* 19, No. 10 (1973), 93–116.

— "Probleme des Menschenbildes in Erzählungen und Novellen (Beitrag zur Geschichte der sozialistisch-realistischen Erzählkunst in der DDR von 1956/57 bis 1963)." Diss. Berlin: Institut für Gesellschaftswissenschaften beim ZK der SED, 1964. [Typescript]

Bräunig, Werner. *Prosa schreiben: Anmerkungen zum Realismus.* Halle/Saale: Mitteldeutscher Verlag, 1968.

Brecht, Bertolt. "Über sozialistischen Realismus." *Neue Deutsche Literatur,* 21, No. 2 (1973), 16.

Brettschneider, Werner. *Zwischen literarischer Autonomie und Staatsdienst: Die Literatur in der DDR.* Berlin: Erich Schmidt, 1972.

Brězan, Jurij. "Geschichten und ihre Erzähler." *Neues Deutschland,* 11 Sept. 1971, p. 4.

Demetz, Peter. *Postwar German Literature: A Critical Introduction.* New York: Pegasus, 1970.

Dietz, Hella. "Die Rede geht von uns." Rev. of *Die anderen und ich,* by Erik Neutsch. *Neue Deutsche Literatur,* 19, No. 2 (1971), 176–82.

"Diskussion um Plenzdorf: Die neuen Leiden des jungen W." *Sinn und Form,* 25 (1973), 219–52.

Dönhoff, Gräfin Marion, Rudolf Walter Leonhardt, Theo Sommer. *Reise in ein fernes Land: Bericht über Kultur, Wirtschaft und Politik in der DDR.* 9th ed. Hamburg: Die Zeit Bücher, 1965.

Doernberg, Stefan. *Kurze Geschichte der DDR.* Berlin: Dietz, 1968.

Drenkow, Renate. "Laudatio auf die kleine Form." *Weimarer Beiträge,* 16, No. 9 (1970), 92–106.

Drewitz, Ingeborg. " 'Sinn und Form' und 'Neue Deutsche Literatur': Notizen zu den letzten Jahrgängen zweier DDR-Zeitschriften." *Neue Deutsche Hefte,* 17, No. 2 (1970), 101–107.

Durzak, Manfred, ed. *Die deutsche Literatur der Gegenwart: Aspekte und Tendenzen.* Stuttgart: Reclam, 1971.

Ebersbach, Volker. "Benito Wogatzki: Der Preis des Mädchens." *Weimarer Beiträge,* 18, No. 9 (1972), 152–57.

Ebert, Günter. "Wirkung und Wagnis: Zum Werk Helmut Sakowskis." *Sinn und Form,* 21 (1969), 1195–1208.

Engels, Friedrich. *Anteil der Arbeit an der Menschwerdung des Affen.* Berlin: Dietz, 1970.

Erkenntnisse und Bekenntnisse. Halle/Saale: Mitteldeutscher Verlag, 1964.

Faber, Elmar and Erhard John, eds. *Das sozialistische Menschenbild: Weg und Wirklichkeit.* 2nd ed. Leipzig: Karl-Marx-Universität, 1968.

Faulseit, Dieter. *Die literarische Erzähltechnik: Eine Einführung.* Beiträge zur Gegenwartsliteratur, 26. Halle/Saale: Verlag Sprache und Literatur, 1963.

Feitknecht, Thomas. *Die sozialistische Heimat: Zum Selbstverständnis neuerer DDR-Romane.* Europäische Hochschulschriften, Reihe 1, vol. 53. Bern: Herbert Lang, 1971.

Flores, John. *Poetry in East Germany: Adjustments, Visions and Provocations, 1945–1970.* New Haven, Con.: Yale Univ. Press, 1971.

Foltin, Hans Friedrich. *Die Unterhaltungsliteratur der DDR.* Ed. Mitteldeutsche Kulturrat e.V. Bonn. Troisdorf: Kammwegverlag, 1970.

Franke, Konrad. *Die Literatur der Deutschen Demokratischen Republik.* Kindlers Literaturgeschichte der Gegenwart in Einzelbänden. München: Kindler, 1971.

Geerdts, Hans Jürgen. "Bemerkungen zur Gestaltung des Menschenbildes in der neuen sozialistischen Epik." *Weimarer Beiträge,* 10 (1964), 105–20.
– ed. *Deutsche Literaturgeschichte in einem Band.* Berlin: Volk und Wissen Volkseigener Verlag, 1971.
– ed. *Literatur der DDR in Einzeldarstellungen.* Kröners Taschenausgabe, 416. Stuttgart: Kröner, 1972.
– *Literatur unserer Zeit.* Wir diskutieren: Eine Schriftenreihe, ed. Fritz Zschech, Heft 8. Rudolstadt: Greifenverlag, 1961.
– "Vielfalt der Handschriften in unserer Prosa." *Neues Deutschland,* 26 July 1972, p. 4.
– "Von der Kunst zu lieben und von der Liebe zur Kunst." Rev. of *Das ungezwungne Leben Kasts,* by Volker Braun. *Neue Deutsche Literatur,* 21, No. 3 (1973), 154–58.
Geisthardt, Hans-Jürgen. "Wahres und Wundersames." Rev. of *Der Mäuseturm,* by Jurij Brězan. *Neue Deutsche Literatur,* 19, No. 8 (1971), 132–35.
"German Writing Today." *Times Literary Supplement,* 23 Sept. 1960, pp. i–xx.
Gorki, Maxim. *Literature and Life: A Selection from the Writings of Maxim Gorki.* Trans. Edith Bone. London: Hutchinson International Authors, 1946.
Gregor-Dellin, Martin. "Mein Stoff ist die Straße: Ein Gespräch mit Manfred Bieler." *Die Zeit,* No. 41, October 1969, pp. 11–12.
Große, Anneliese. "Vom Werden des Menschen: Zum Werk Franz Fühmanns." *Weimarer Beiträge,* 17, No. 1 (1971), 54–78.
Güsten, Michael O. "Prolegomena zu einer Metaphysik des positiven Helden." *Neue Deutsche Literatur,* 4, No. 5 (1956), 162–63.
Hager, Kurt. *Grundfragen des geistigen Lebens im Sozialismus: Referat auf der 10. Tagung des ZK der SED, 28./29.4.1969.* Berlin: Dietz, 1969.
Hartinger, Walfried and Klaus Werner. "Zur Konfliktgestaltung in der sozialistisch-realistischen Literatur und Kunst." *Weimarer Beiträge,* 18, No. 9 (1972), 119–30.
Henniger, Gerhard. "Für eine höhere Wirksamkeit unserer Literatur im Leben des Volkes." *Weimarer Beiträge,* 17, No. 12 (1971), 5–9.
Herber, Christa. "Sozialistische Persönlichkeit und Kunst." *Weimarer Beiträge,* 17, No. 9 (1971), 23–39.
Herting, Helga. "Zum Heldischen in der sozialistisch-realistischen Literatur." *Weimarer Beiträge,* 15, Sonderheft (1969), 205–219.
– *Das sozialistische Menschenbild in der Gegenwartsliteratur: Beiträge zur Kunsterziehung.* Berlin: Verlag Tribüne, 1966.
Heyden, Günter. "Persönlichkeit und Gemeinschaft in der sozialistischen Gesellschaft." *Deutsche Zeitschrift für Philosophie,* 16, No. 1 (1968), 6–37.
Hinweise für schreibende Arbeiter. Leipzig: Verlag für Buch- und Bibliothekswesen, 1961.
Hochmuth, Arno. "Zum Problem der Massenwirksamkeit unserer Gegenwartsliteratur." *Weimarer Beiträge,* 17, No. 10 (1971), 10–18.
Huebener, Theodore. *The Literature of East Germany.* New York: Ungar, 1970.
Ilberg, Werner. "Ferment gegen Lauheit?" Rev. of *Er kam mit dem Herbstwind,* by Martin Selber. *Neue Deutsche Literatur,* 19, No. 2 (1971), 182–84.
Jäckel, Günter. "Zwischen Erinnerungen und Vertrauen." *Neue Deutsche Literatur,* 20, No. 1 (1972), 135–44.
Jarmatz, Klaus, ed. *Kritik in der Zeit: Der Sozialismus – seine Literatur – ihre Entwicklung.* Halle/Saale: Mitteldeutscher Verlag, 1970.
Jehser, Werner. "Zum neuen Charakter des literarischen Konflikts." *Weimarer Beiträge,* 16, No. 2 (1970), 82–107.
Jendryschik, Manfred. "Was kann eine Kurzgeschichte leisten? Mit dem Autor sprach Armin Zeißler." *Sonntag,* No. 39, (1971), p. 7.

Joho, Wolfgang. "Notwendiges Streitgespräch: Bemerkungen zu einem internationalen Kolloquium." *Neue Deutsche Literatur*, 13, No. 3 (1965), 88–112.

Kant, Uwe. "Bräunigs gewöhnliche Geschichten" Rev. of *Gewöhnliche Leute*, by Werner Bräunig. *Neue Deutsche Literatur*, 17, No. 12 (1969), 144–48.

Keßler, Horst and Fred Staufenbiel et al., eds. *Kultur in unserer Zeit: Zur Theorie und Praxis der sozialistischen Kulturrevolution in der DDR*. Berlin: Dietz, under the auspices of the Institut für Gesellschaftswissenschaften beim ZK der SED, 1965.

Klein, Eduard. "Bild und Menschenbild." *Neue Deutsche Literatur*, 15, No. 6 (1967), 3–7.

Köhler, Willi. "Ein Dramatiker erzählt Geschichten" Rev. of *Zwei Zentner Leichtigkeit*, by Helmut Sakowski. *Neue Deutsche Literatur*, 19, No. 1 (1971), 176–78.

"Die Kraft des moralischen Konflikts." *Sonntag*, 29 Nov. 1970, pp. 4–5.

"Kultur der Arbeit – Kultur der Umwelt." *Sonntag*, 19 July 1970, pp. 3–4.

Kultur-Politisches Wörterbuch. Berlin: Dietz, 1970.

Kunert, Günter. "Manche, Einige, Gewisse und Sogenannte." *Sinn und Form*, 24 (1972), 1099–1104.

Kurella, Alfred. *Das Eigene und das Fremde: Neue Beiträge zum sozialistischen Humanismus*. 2nd ed., rev. Berlin: Aufbau-Verlag, 1970.

– *Der Mensch als Schöpfer seiner selbst: Beiträge zum sozialistischen Humanismus*. Berlin: Aufbau-Verlag, 1961.

Kurzweg, Volker. "Interview mit Helmut Sakowski." *Weimarer Beiträge*, 15, No. 4 (1969), 742–51.

Leistner, Bernd. "Der Epiker Johannes Bobrowski." Diss. Leipzig: Sektion Kulturwissenschaften und Germanistik, 1971. [Typescript]

Literaturkunde: Beiträge zu Wesen und Formen der Dichtung. 3rd ed. Leipzig: Fachbuchverlag, 1965.

Loose, Gerhard. "Grundbegriffe des sozialistischer [sic] Realismus." *Monatshefte*, 57, No. 4 (1965), 162–70.

Marx, Karl and Friedrich Engels. *Über Kunst und Literatur in zwei Bänden*. Vol. 1. Berlin: Dietz, 1967.

– *Werke*. Vols. 1–39. Berlin: Dietz, 1959–68.

Mayer, Hans. *Deutsche Literatur seit Thomas Mann*. rororo Taschenbuch Ausgabe, 1063. Reinbek bei Hamburg: Rowohlt, 1968.

Mittenzwei, Werner and Reinhard Weisbach, eds. *Revolution und Literatur: Zum Verhältnis von Erbe, Revolution und Literatur*. Frankfurt am Main: Röderberg Taschenbuch, 1972.

Mühlberg, Dietrich. "Kulturarbeit und Persönlichkeit." *Weimarer Beiträge*, 17, No. 9 (1971), 5–10.

Müller-Sternberg, R. "Rezensionen: Milovan Djilas: *Die unvollkommene Gesellschaft: jenseits der 'Neuen Klasse'*...." *Deutsche Studien*, 7, No. 27 (1969) 324–25.

Nahke, Evamaria. "Arbeit an den großen Gegenständen unserer Zeit: Gespräch mit Benito Wogatzki." *Weimarer Beiträge*, 15, No. 4 (1969), 723–41.

Nalewski, Horst. *Sprachkünstlerische Gestaltung: Stilkritische Anmerkungen zur jüngeren Epik*. Halle/Saale: Mitteldeutscher Verlag, 1968.

Neubert, Werner. "Geschichten vom Heute." Rev. of *Der Preis des Mädchens und andere Erzählungen*, by Benito Wogatzki. *Neue Deutsche Literatur*, 20, No. 1 (1972), 144–46.

– "Meister Falk und die anderen: Ein Diskussionsbeitrag." Interview with Benito Wogatzki. *Neue Deutsche Literatur*, 16, No. 8 (1968), 13–28.

– "Das neue Menschenbild: Wirklichkeit und Wirkung." *Neue Deutsche Literatur*, 16, No. 1 (1968), 4–13.

– "Niete in Hosen – oder ...?" Rev. of *Die neuen Leiden des jungen W.*, by Ulrich Plenzdorf. *Neue Deutsche Literatur*, 21, No. 3 (1973), 130–35.

— "Unsere Konflikte in unserer Literatur." *Neue Deutsche Literatur,* 18, No. 1 (1970), 5—13.

Neugebauer, Heinz. *Anna Seghers: Ihr Leben und Werk.* Schriftsteller der Gegenwart. Berlin: Volk und Wissen Volkseigener Verlag, 1970.

Nowojski, Walter. "Interview mit Erwin Strittmatter." *Neue Deutsche Literatur,* 13, No. 6 (1965), 65—66.

Pedderson, Jan. "Die literarische Situation in der DDR." In *Handbuch der deutschen Gegenwartsliteratur.* Ed. Hermann Kunisch. München: Nymphenburger Verlagshandlung, 1965, pp. 746—58.

Plavius, Heinz. "Freuden an Leiden." *Sinn und Form,* 25 (1973), 448—53.

— "Gespräch mit Werner Heiduczek." Interview with Werner Heiduczek. *Neue Deutsche Literatur,* 19, No. 8 (1971), 19—23.

— "Gestalt und Gestaltung . . ." Rev. of *Glas und Ahorn,* by Manfred Jendryschik, and of *Labyrinth ohne Schrecken,* by Joachim Nowotny. *Neue Deutsche Literatur,* 15, No. 3 (1968), 148—58.

— "Literatur als Indiz." *Sinn und Form,* 22 (1970), 1516—22.

— "Der positive Held im sozialistischen Realismus und der neue Charakter der Arbeit." *Deutsche Zeitschrift für Philosophie,* 11, No. 8 (1963), 933—55.

Pracht, Erwin and Werner Neubert, eds. *Sozialistischer Realismus — Positionen, Probleme, Perspektiven: Eine Einführung.* Berlin: Dietz, 1970.

Raddatz, Fritz J. "DDR-Literatur und Marxistische Ästhetik." *Germanic Review,* 43, No. 1 (1968), 40—60.

— ed. *Marxismus und Literatur: Eine Dokumentation in drei Bänden.* Vols. I—III. Reinbek bei Hamburg: Rowohlt, 1969.

— *Traditionen und Tendenzen: Materialien zur Literatur der DDR.* Frankfurt am Main: Suhrkamp, 1972.

Rammler, Michael. "Vom moralischen Nutzen künstlerischer Aneignung." *Weimarer Beiträge,* 17, No. 9 (1971), 40—62.

Reich-Ranicki, Marcel. *Deutsche Literatur in West und Ost: Prosa seit 1945.* München: Piper, 1963.

Reichel, Peter. "Rauhbein oder Außenseiter? " *Forum: Organ des Zentralrats der FDJ,* 26, No. 16 (1972), 13.

Richter, Hans. "Daß der Mensch dem Menschen ein Helfer ist . . . : Zum Menschenbild in neuen Erzählwerken der DDR." *Weimarer Beiträge,* 15, No. 5 (1969), 1056—75.

Richter, Helmut. "Begegnung mit Joachim Nowotny."*Sonntag,* 22 Feb. 1970, p. 16.

Röhner, Eberhard. *Abschied, Ankunft und Bewährung: Entwicklungsprobleme unserer sozialistischen Literatur.* Berlin: Dietz, 1969.

— *Arbeiter in der Gegenwartsliteratur.* Berlin: Dietz, 1967.

Rothbauer, Gerhard. "Vorgeschichten, Nachgeschichten oder einfach Geschichten? " Rev. of *Vorgeschichten oder Schöne Gegend Probstein,* by Helga Schütz. *Neue Deutsche Literatur,* 20, No. 1 (1972), 163—66.

— "Wie sich die 'verborgene Sache' beim Erzählen offenbart." Rev. of *Sonntag unter Leuten,* by Joachim Nowotny. *Neue Deutsche Literatur,* 19, No. 8 (1971), 135—41.

Rühle, Jürgen. *Literatur und Revolution: Die Schriftsteller und der Kommunismus.* Köln: Kiepenheuer and Witsch, 1960.

Sauter, Josef-Hermann. "Interview mit Franz Fühmann." *Weimarer Beiträge,* 17, No. 1 (1971), 33—53.

Scheler, Hermann. "Die Dialektik von gesellschaftlichem Gesamtwillen und Einzelwillen der sozialistischen Persönlichkeit." *Deutsche Zeitschrift für Philosophie,* 16, No. 10, (1968), 1165—90.

Schlenstedt, Dieter. "Ankunft und Anspruch: Zum neueren Roman in der DDR." *Sinn und Form*, 18, (1966), 814–35.

– "Zu Problemen des Menschenbildes in der jüngsten sozialistischen Romanliteratur." *Weimarer Beiträge*, 8, No. 3 (1962), 509–40.

Schlenstedt, Silvia. "Volker Braun: Das ungezwungne Leben Kasts." Rev. of *Das ungezwungne Leben Kasts*, by Volker Braun. *Weimarer Beiträge*, 19, No. 3 (1973), 136–43.

Schonauer, Franz. "DDR auf dem Bitterfelder Weg." *Neue Deutsche Hefte*, 13, No. 1 (1966), 91–117.

Schubbe, Elimar, ed. *Dokumente zur Kunst-, Literatur-Kulturpolitik der SED.* Stuttgart: Seewald, 1972.

Schwarze, Hanns Werner. *DDR heute.* Köln: Kiepenheuer and Witsch, 1970.

– *Die DDR ist keine Zone mehr.* Köln: Kiepenheuer and Witsch, 1969.

Seghers, Anna. *Über Kunstwerk und Wirklichkeit.* Ed. and introduced by Sigrid Bock. Deutsche Bibliothek, Studienausgaben zur neueren deutschen Literatur, 3 vols. Berlin: Akademie Verlag, 1970–71.

Simons, Elizabeth. " 'Das Andersmachen, von Grund auf': Die Hauptrichtung der jüngsten erzählenden DDR-Literatur." *Weimarer Beiträge*, 15, Sonderheft (1969), 183–204.

Simon, Horst. "Was Erzählungen Neues Entdecken." *Neues Deutschland,* 25 June 1972, p. 4.

Sommer, Dietrich. " 'Die anderen und ich' im Erzählwerk von Erik Neutsch." *Weimarer Beiträge*, 19, No. 9 (1973), 108–116.

– "Interview mit Erik Neutsch." *Weimarer Beiträge*, 19, No. 9 (1973), 99–107.

Sozialistische Beziehungen in Familien und Hausgemeinschaften bewußter Gestalten: Materialien der Sitzung des Verfassungs- und Rechtsausschusses der Volkskammer der DDR vom 24. Februar 1971. Heft 21, Fünfte Wahlperiode. [n.p.]: Abteilung Presse und Information des Staatsrates der Deutschen Demokratischen Republik, 1971.

Steinhaußen, Ursula, Dieter Faulseit, Jürgen Bonk, eds. *Handbuch für schreibende Arbeiter.* Berlin: Verlag Tribüne, 1969.

Thomas, Karin. "Die Literatur der DDR als Spiegel von Gesellschaftsbewußtsein und Gesellschaftskritik." In *Wissenschaft und Gesellschaft in der DDR,* ed. Peter Christian Ludz. München: Hanser, 1971, pp. 156–84.

Timofejew, L. I. "Über amerikanische Kritiken zur Sowjetliteratur." In *Falschmünzer der Literatur: Zur Kritik bürgerlicher und revisionistischer Literaturanschauungen.* Berlin: Dietz, 1962, pp. 126–46.

Wallmann, Jürgen P. *Argumente: Informationen und Meinungen zur deutschen Literatur der Gegenwart: Aufsätze und Kritiken.* Mühlacker: Stieglitz, 1968.

Walther, Joachim. "Autoren-Werkstatt: Irmtraud Morgner." *Weltbühne*, 47, 8 Aug. 1972, 1010–13.

Wangenheim, Inge von. *Die Geschichte und unsere Geschichten: Gedanken eines Schriftstellers auf der Suche nach den Fabeln seiner Zeit.* Halle/Saale: Mitteldeutscher Verlag, 1968.

– *Die Verschwörung der Musen: Gedanken eines Schriftstellers auf der Suche nach der Methode seiner Zeit.* Halle/Saale: Mitteldeutscher Verlag, 1971.

Wilpert, Gero von. *Sachwörterbuch der Literatur.* 5th ed., rev. Kröners Taschenausgabe, 531. Stuttgart: Kröner, 1969.

Wolf, Christa. *Lesen und Schreiben: Aufsätze und Betrachtungen.* Edition Neue Texte. Berlin: Aufbau-Verlag, 1972.

– "Vorwort." In *Larifari und andere Erzählungen,* by Juri Kasakow. 2nd ed. Berlin: Verlag Kultur und Fortschritt, 1967, pp. 5–11.

"Wortmeldung: Schriftsteller über Erfahrungen, Pläne und Probleme." *Neue Deutsche Literatur,* 19, No. 1 (1971), 29–70.

Wyniger, Willy. *Demokratie und Plan in der DDR: Probleme der Bewältigung der wissenschaftlich-technischen Revolution.* Sammlung Junge Wissenschaft. Köln: Pahl-Rugenstein, 1971.

Zimmermann, Werner. *Deutsche Prosadichtungen unseres Jahrhunderts: Interpretationen für Lehrende und Lernende.* Vol. 2. Düsseldorf: Pädagog. Verlag Schwann, 1969.

Unpublished Sources:

Gumtau, Helmut. "Schriftsteller-Vortrupp oder Nachhut? DDR-Literatur heute: Vortrag." Berlin [West], Spring 1972, pp. 1–17.

Wolf, Christa. "Christa Wolf liest aus 'Nachdenken über Christa T.': Zu Beginn ein Gespräch mit der Schriftstellerin über die Arbeit an der Erzählung." Berliner Rundfunk [Ost], 18 Oct. 1966.